STUDIES
IN
II TIMOTHY

STUDIES
IN
II TIMOTHY

by

H. C. G. Moule

KREGEL PUBLICATIONS
Grand Rapids, Michigan 49501

STUDIES IN SECOND TIMOTHY, published in 1977, by Kregel
Publications, a division of Kregel, Inc. All rights reserved.

Library of Congress Cataloging in Publication Data

Moule, Handley Carr Glyn, Bp. of Durham, 1841-1920.
  Studies in Second Timothy.

  (Kregel Popular Commentary Series)
  Reprint of the ed. published by Religious Tract
Society, London, under title: The second epistle to
Timothy, in series: A devotional commentary.
  1. Bible. N.T. 2 Timothy — Commentaries.
I. Moule, Handley Carr Glyn, Bp. of Durham, 1841-1920.
II. Title.   III. Series: A Devotional commentary.
BS2743.M68   1977   227'.84'07   77-79182
ISBN 0-8254-3219-7

Printed in the United States of America

CONTENTS

Contents

PREFATORY NOTE

THE purpose and the method of this book are both so simple that no more than a 'Note' is befitting by way of Introduction.

The writer has taken up this heart-moving Epistle with the single intention of expounding it after the manner of a 'Bible Reading,' not for literary criticism or enquiry but in quest of divine messages for heart and life.

Personal attention to the very words of Holy Scripture, in the spirit of obedience and prayer, was never more needed in the Christian Church than now. Happy will the writer be if by producing a modest specimen of such study he may promote its exercise by others.

H. C. G. MOULE

LIGHT after darkness, gain after loss,
Strength after suffering, crown after cross,
Sweet after bitter, song after sigh,
Home after wandering, praise after cry ;

Sheaves after sowing, sun after rain,
Sight after mystery, peace after pain,
Joy after sorrow, calm after blast,
Rest after weariness, sweet rest at last.

F. R. H.

1

THE EPISTLE:
ITS DATE AND CIRCUMSTANCES

LET us read together the Second Epistle of St. Paul Our Method to Timothy. The method of our study shall be the of Study simplest possible. After some brief introductory views of the Epistle and of the probable conditions of its production we will take it up verse by verse, passage by passage, for examination first of the language, then of the messages carried by means of it to the soul and to the Church.

The reader will not find, here in the introductions Certain As- or later in the comments, anything like elaborate sumptions criticism of the purely literary sort. Whatever be the place for that (and abundant occasion for it has been found in modern times in connexion with the Letters to Timothy and Titus), that place is not here, where we meet in spiritual companionship for believing medi- tation. I approach this precious 'dying Letter' with certain formed and settled convictions about it, and these I shall treat in our present study as assumed to be true. For example, I am entirely convinced, and I shall assume this as a fact in my comments, that the Letter is the genuine production of St. Paul. I am convinced that it was written by him, or more pre- cisely dictated by him to the faithful Luke (iv. 11), in a Roman prison, not very long before the death of the author as a martyr for his Lord. This took place

The Second Epistle to Timothy

at a time, so I feel amply assured, some few years later than that last mention of St. Paul at the close of the Acts (xxviii. 30, 31) where we see him 'in his own hired house,' or rather lodging; spending 'two whole years' there, in captivity indeed, but able all the time to be busy about the beloved work of his life as a missionary of Jesus Christ. I take it to be certain that he was permitted at the end of that time to quit Rome a free man; that he traversed seas and lands again as of old, perhaps even as far as distant Spain; that he laboured almost to the last in evangelization and in the arrangement and settlement of the mission-churches around the Mediterranean shores; and that at length he was again arrested, somewhere in Asia Minor, perhaps at Troas; carried to Rome, rigorously imprisoned, and finally, after a public trial, condemned and put to death.

Partly traditions old enough and sober enough to command our confidence, partly the internal evidence afforded by these three Pastoral Epistles, or Letters to Pastors, and by this Letter in particular, seem to me to put this general conclusion upon a safe footing.

The Date As to the date more precisely when our Letter was written, we may reasonably place it within the years 66 or 67. The time, so the contents clearly indicate, was a time of terror and danger; persecution was in the air. 'All men forsook' the lonely Apostle (iv. 16); far different from that earlier day when 'no man forbade him' to 'receive all that came unto him' to hear the message of life. His temporary respite from sentence (iv. 17) is described as a 'deliverance out of the lion's mouth.' One faithful friend, and

10

only one, was always at his side (iv. 11). Everything speaks of the shadows of danger and of death, everything indicates that he was used with a severity unknown before. We can scarcely err therefore in assigning the Letter to some time within the last dreadful years of the reign (54-68) of Nero, perhaps soon after that outburst of cruel warfare upon Christianity which began when (66) the wretched Emperor set fire to the City and then turned the popular anger against the suspected and hated Christians.

If so, we may in some measure illustrate the then **The Church** feeling of the public towards the converts and their **as it seemed** Apostle by what in our times would be felt by society **to the** in its alarm towards some real or supposed nihilist **Pagans** plot against existing institutions, and particularly towards its suspected leader. It was very much as a nihilistic secret community that the Christian Church was actually viewed by credulous and frightened pagan opinion in Rome; so we know from the Latin historians. Allegiance to the Lord Jesus was taken to mean high treason to the State, and the 'conversation in heaven' was represented as a 'hatred of the human race.'

To realize this is to appreciate, however weakly, the awfulness of the cloud which, from the human point of view, brooded, full of sullen thunders, over the head of St. Paul when he wrote this dying Letter. With that realization present we shall read its utterances of sadness with the more reverent sympathy, and we shall wonder and worship the more over its words of 'everlasting comfort and good hope through grace.'

2

TIMOTHY AND HIS POSITION

Our reflections thus far have led us to recall the darkness, the awfulness, of the probable time and conditions of the writing of the Epistle, as they regarded the Writer. We may follow the same thought out with its Receiver in our view.

Timothy What do we know of Timothy, as he stood then in face of life and labour, of duty and sorrow? His name is abundantly familiar to us from the Acts, and from repeated mentions by St. Paul in his Epistles. The earliest mention comes to us in Acts xvi. 1, where we read of his Gentile father and Jewish mother, the Eunice of this Epistle (i. 5). The latest mention is before us here. From the time when St Paul first adopted him as his personal missionary helper (say in 51 or 52) till now, when he is the superintending Pastor of the great Ephesian mission, Timothy appears as labouring always in close and endeared connexion with St. Paul, 'as son with father' (Phil. ii. 22). Their characters would seem to have exactly tended to draw their hearts and affections together. On the one side was the Apostle, in whom were wonderfully blended a supreme strength of purpose and a far - seeing natural genius with exquisite sensibilities and sympathies and a love-welcoming heart. On the other side was his spiritual 'son,' like him in a devotion, deep as the soul, to the

12

name and cause of the Lord Jesus, while manifestly
unlike him in a character (we cannot mistake it as
we trace the fine unconscious touches of allusive
description in the Epistles, *e.g.* 1 Cor. xvi. 10, 11),
shy and sensitive even to timidity, anxious in the
face of difficult duty, clinging to a stronger personality
than his own, born rather to second—with a noble
fidelity—than to lead. Such likenesses and such
differences would together draw those hearts into a
friendship of the tenderest and deepest, when once
Christ had made them one. The strong man would
find a joy and solace in the devotion to him of the
less strong. The younger man and weaker would
feel as if the presence, or at least the knowledge
of the life and possible presence, of his glorious yet
most humanly tender chief constituted the inmost
light and power of his being, under God. Joined to
each other in the Lord, with that peculiarly strong
and holy bond which links the converter to the
converted, the helper to the helped, they would need
each other, meet each other, bless each other, in a
thousand ways.

And now, in the year 66 or 67, what aspect does His dark
life take for Timothy? He stands at the darkest Hour
hour of all his day. He has been doing his best for
some while to be leader, not follower, under his dear
'Father's' commission. He has been trying, so the
First Epistle informs us, to act as ministerial and
administrative head of the Ephesian mission with its
many daughter-missions around it; a task far less to
his soul's liking, we may be sure, than the happy
simplicity of taking and doing, one by one, the orders

The Second Epistle to Timothy

of a beloved chief. He has had the pain, the strain, the solitary and anxious trouble, for such it would be to him, of standing alone and in the front; tasting the dreariness of a prominence for which he felt no natural gift. This would be a sad experience at any time for a Timothy; but what would it be at a crisis when the Neronian terror grew daily more formidable, and when to be prominent among the hated Christians was to be marked for probable destruction? Then, on the other hand, just then, under just that strain of circumstance, apparently in and from Timothy's very presence, while he wept an agony of tears (i. 4), St. Paul, who had joined him for a time, was torn from him by the police or soldiers of the persecutor and carried out and away for martyrdom. Who that has the least power to feel through the heart of another does not ache with some sense of that agony as he thinks upon it? It was death in life to a Timothy. The burthened mind and the broken heart were blent into one dreadful consciousness of blind distress. Timothy stood awfully lonely, yet awfully exposed, in face of a world of thronging sorrows. Well might he have been shaken to the root of his faith. He might almost have tasted a drop of that last despair which gives up God and wishes that being could cease to be.

To such a heart, when some sad weeks had passed away, came this Letter, our Second Epistle to Timothy, to pour its mighty sympathies into his sorrow and to bid him be strong again in the living Lord Jesus Christ.

Christian reader, do you know what great grief

14

means? Do 'the clouds return after the rain,' even more heavy than before, upon your lot? 'The Bible knows all about it.' Its saints have tasted this cup before you. And now through their pains, and through their long eternal peace, the Book says to you that a great and wonderful joy is on its way towards you to end the night, 'coming in the morning.'

3

THE CRISIS OF THE CHURCH

WE have seen something of the human sorrows, deep and possessing, which beset the heart of the Writer of this Letter and the heart of its Receiver. The same subject must claim our attention a little longer, and now from another point of view.

The pangs of heart which we have thus far thought of have been chiefly personal. St. Paul has moved before us as the man called to taste the cup of desertion, of abominable suspicions and false charges, and of an unjust consignment to death. In Timothy we have seen the man loaded with the weight, laid upon shoulders of no heroic strength, of a great public pastoral care along with a broken heart. But with all this there was assigned to them both another and most mournful trial, the trial of the apparent failure of their sacred Cause. I mean that to every **The Gospel** eye but that of faith it must have appeared just then **in apparent** as if the Gospel were on the eve of extinction. **Peril** When things look black to every eye but that of faith, there comes necessarily the severest possible trial to faith, constituted as our nature is. And when faith is so tried the Christian realizes indeed how dark darkness can be.

Think what it must have seemed in those evil days when at last the forces of the Roman State, largely influenced by the worst of heathen autocrats, were

16

turned against Christianity. From one point of view no doubt the Gospel had made wonderful progress within the thirty-five years or so since it set out from Pentecost. But seen from another side, what a feeble, what a tentative cause it was! The converts were still a 'little flock,' very little, compared to the masses of the population. We may illustrate their position not unfairly by what the disciples of the Reformation were in Spain in the middle of the sixteenth century. The Spanish Reformation had been a remarkable movement; it had won numerous adherents, not least among the upper classes. Yet it was relatively a small thing amidst the great mass of Spaniards. Then the dominant power, armed with the tremendous Inquisition, took its suppression in hand— and it was suppressed. In the mystery of God's permission the dread adverse force 'made war upon the saints, *and overcame them*' (Rev. xiii. 7). The weak succumbed absolutely to the strong, and for many long generations the Gospel light in its purity was practically quenched in Spain.

An Illustration [marginal note]

There was nothing from the natural outlook to tell Paul and Timothy at the crisis before us that a suppression quite as complete as this was not awaiting the very existence of the Church of Christ. The Roman Empire was intolerant of secret societies, and it knew how to extinguish them. In its view Christianity was a very dangerous secret society, and it was a secret society with no material forces at its command. It could be suppressed; it was to be suppressed; the statesman, the despot, the fanatic, were all agreed upon it. And now the far most

The Second Epistle to Timothy

important leader of the society was in prison, and would soon in fact be dead.

An agonis-
ing Trial to
Faith
We are so habituated to Christianity as being, apart from its divine character, a vast factor in the modern world that it needs an effort to realize that when this Epistle was written it trembled, *humanly speaking*, on the verge of annihilation. Did Paul, did Timothy, never half ask themselves if it would not be annihilated in fact? We may be sure that they did. And their only answer would be, not a calculated forecast of probabilities, but a grasp, strong as death while full of the life of faith, upon the Lord Jesus Christ. And that grasp would be no facile act of instinct. They 'groaned, being burthened,' while they overcame. It cost them an agony to 'gird up their loins, and to hope to the end.'

'Behold, we count them happy that endure.' And we are not only to count them happy, but to follow them, by like paths, so far as God wills it for us, to the same deep and ever-living happiness. For us too, in our Christian course to-day, unless we are strangely insensible to facts around us, there hang thunder-clouds enough and to spare in the sky of the Church. Invasions by the world from without, confusions and strifes within, doubts, heresies, superstitions, an indifference 'heavy as frost'—these are some of our 'unfavourable conditions.' It is a moment of suspense and shadows. Well, let us again remember that 'the Bible knows all about it.' And let us learn from the page which tells us so that it 'knows' also the one sure secret of victory; not clever forecasts but an invincible personal reliance:—'I KNOW WHOM I HAVE BELIEVED.'

4

THE WITNESS OF THE EPISTLE
TO ITSELF

ACTING on my initial explanation I have offered no technical discussion of literary and historical problems in connexion with our Epistle. I have simply expressed my convictions, and have asked the reader rather to take them for granted for the while than to listen to arguments over the authentic Pauline authorship.

I modify this rule at this point just so far as to say a few words on one item of internal evidence to that authorship which to my own mind is as weighty as possible. It has everything to do with what we have been thinking in regard of the heart-sorrows of Paul and of Timothy, and the trials to their faith.

As a fact, the Letters to Timothy and to Titus, after having been accepted as authentic without misgiving throughout the ages, have been, within the nineteenth century, severely and in many quarters, doubted or denied to be St. Paul's. Modern Doubts about the Pastoral Epistles Many acute students, some of them far from irreverent in spirit, have taken this line. It has been said in particular that the style of expression is seriously unlike that of the Apostle's other Letters; that the state of church-organization shewn in them is too advanced for his time; that it is impossible to fit them into his biography, supposing that biography to close with the close of the Acts of the Apostles.

I believe that every one of these difficulties may be

accounted for while we maintain the authenticity of the Letters—except indeed the last. As to that last, I admit that it is impossible to find a credible place for the three ' Pastorals ' within the narrative of the Acts. But can any reasonable student think that the writer of the Acts means us to understand that St Paul died at the end of the 'two whole years in his own hired house'? Rather, is there not ground for the guess (by Professor Ramsay, if I remember aright) that St. Luke intended *a third volume* to follow, a sequel to his Gospel and to the Acts, but that God willed otherwise, and that the narrative accordingly closes abruptly, short of its goal? If so, there is left ample room for an after-time in which to place the 'Pastorals'; and that class of objection falls accordingly.

The Evidence of the Human Heart

But all this leaves untouched the internal evidence to which I now point. Few students doubt that these three Epistles, authentic or not, stand or fall together ; so curiously, so amply are they alike in their indefinable literary character and *air*. If one stands therefore, all stand together. Now this Second Epistle to Timothy stands, with a standing, as I maintain, immovable, upon the evidence borne by that inimitable accent of the sorrow-burthened human soul which sounds all throughout its utterances. I have often found it difficult deliberately to read these short chapters through without finding something like a mist gathering in the eyes. The writer's heart beats in the writing. You can almost see his tears fall over the dear past and the harrowing present. Meanwhile a noble gravity, the very tone of the man who knows that he is on his way to death, and that he must say his last words clearly and decisively, now or never, suffuses the whole composition. The writer is alternately strong with the resolute man's last calm courage, and tender as a yearning and solitary woman when he begs the beloved one to whom he writes to 'come to him,' if he possibly can, 'before winter,' because he is so awfully alone.

Now here is an element which, I am bold to say, in a writing produced within the first generations of Christianity, cannot but indicate an absolute authenticity. I appeal to those who know the history of literature, especially to those who have given attention to attempts at elaborate imitation preserved in the literature of antiquity. I ask them whether they think that anyone, in Christian circles, within, let us say, one hundred and fifty years of the death of our Lord, was in the least likely to have made not merely a passable imitation of an apostolic letter in *some* style, but an imitation in *this* style. Was there a genius within those circles at once so deep, so tender, and so perverted, as to have fabricated such sentences as these?—'I am mindful of thy tears'; 'I know whom I have believed'; 'At my first answer all men forsook me; nevertheless the Lord stood by me, and strengthened me.' But to quote even such sentences in their isolation is not enough; we must read the Letter over. *The human heart* is in it everywhere. And fabricators, certainly of that age, did not well understand the human heart.

It is Paul himself; the original, the authentic *man*. And in Paul was JESUS CHRIST. Then let us read, let us listen, let us believe. We shall find the dying Letter full of living messages, carried to us by a sure messenger's hand, direct from HIM.

Could Fabrication invent this Tone?

5

SAINT PAUL

2 Timothy 1: 1,2

PAUL, an apostle of Jesus Christ by the will of God, according to the promise of life which is in Christ Jesus, to Timothy, *my* dearly beloved son : Grace, mercy, and peace, from God the Father and Christ Jesus our Lord. A.V.

—————

Paul, apostle of Christ Jesus, through the will of God, according to the promise of the life which is in Christ Jesus, to Timothy, beloved child, grace, mercy, peace, from God the Father and Christ Jesus our Lord.

2 Tim. i. 1, 2.
The two Friends in the Prison

So begins this most wonderful of farewells. We seem to see the two figures in the twilight of the Roman vault, Paul as he dictates and Luke as he writes down the words on the papyrus sheet before him. For this Letter assuredly, if any of the apostle's messages, was dictated ; what else could he do in that half-darkness, with eyes probably never strong and now more than ever dim with use and grief ? Once more, yet this once more, he will employ his old skill and set his secretary to work. Once more the familiar opening syllables shall be spoken and written, and the communication in due form begun.

The Signature

We moderns *close* our letters with our signed names. In the old days it was the other way ; the sender's name was the first word written. I notice this now only to remind the reader that such an opening then was as little formal as are our endings

Saint Paul

now. To us the style reads somewhat official and distant:—'*Paul, Apostle.*' It recalls to us documents of the legal and ceremonial order in which potentates and dignitaries address us from aloft, gravely reciting their names and styles. It is worth while accordingly to recollect that, when St. Paul lived and wrote, the most familiar correspondence would open in this way. True, he cannot help imparting to his writing a solemn dignity proper to the messenger and the friend of JESUS; but for all this the writing is cast in a form which is the absolutely natural expression of the heart of the loving father to his own dear child. 2 Tim. i. 1, 2.

As we pause a moment over that wonderful name of PAUL, let us once more thank God that it does as a fact denote for us just this—so deep, so vivid, so human a personality. Who of all the saints of the Bible is more the living man to us than this same Paul? He is to us as if we had seen his face, and touched his hand, and caught the accent of his voice, and detected the tears in his tired eyes. We have come to feel that we know him in his splendid strength; in his strength of nature, shewn in an intellect, a will, a love, an indignation, of the highest kind; in his strength of grace, 'the power of Christ overarching him' (2 Cor. xii. 9); 'Christ magnified in his body' (Phil. i. 20); so that indeed the LORD looked from his eyes, spoke from his lips, moved and acted in his behaviour; 'not he, but Christ' (Gal. ii. 20). We have come also to feel that we know St. Paul through the heart-moving attraction of his weaknesses; his bodily weaknesses, The name Paul

23

The Second Epistle to Timothy

so often alluded to by himself or by others, and which seem sometimes to have taken forms and degrees of even agonizing distress; and then also those weaknesses of the soul, if weaknesses they can be called, which laid open his deep sensibilities to every blow inflicted by his own sorrows and anxieties, and by those of others. This is the PAUL who now once more sets down his personal name at the head of a letter, a letter which is to utter all his heart.

Revelation through Personality

What has this reflection to say to us? Surely this at least, that it is a peculiar and precious feature of the New Testament revelation, not to speak now of that of the Old, that it comes to us so largely through the sacred channel of the human heart, the human personality. It does not descend in oracular thunder from the clouds. It is conveyed in great measure through a series of Letters, signed with men's names, and speaking in the dialect of man's soul, and now particularly in the dialect of *this* man's soul, a soul so deeply capacious of grief, of hope, of weariness, of eagerness, of longing and of love.

Let us approach such a section of the Book of Truth with no less reverence and submission for this thought; for we reflect that this man, who bears this dear familiar name, is the 'Chosen Vessel,' the actual Delegate of the Christ of God. But let our submission be made at once all the tenderer and all the stronger by the thought that the Christ of God used that Chosen Vessel as no mere mechanical vehicle. He took and employed for His sacred purpose the whole wonderful nature,

24

the whole living and radiating personality. He 2 Tim. i. wielded for us the whole complex world of His 1, 2. servant's deep experiences of toil and pain. He spoke to us not through His servant's lips only but through his heart, aye, through his suffering, broken, yet believing heart.

How long the saint has rested now from all that was sorrowful in that use and service! How fully he rejoices now in the mighty privilege of having been so employed, even to the most sensitive depth of his being, for that beloved Lord!

Shall we not ask that we too, in our little measure, may be willing from the soul to be likewise at the service of that same Possessor, till we too rest and are 'comforted' in His presence above?

6

THE APOSTLE OF CHRIST JESUS

2 Timothy 1: 1

So the Writer of the Letter has passed before us as the living man, the sufferer of pain and sorrow, carrying with him to the last hour all that is implied in a living personality, and used in all the range of his conscious being to be the Chosen Vessel to bear Another's name.

Christianity and the Person

Let us pause yet a moment to reflect upon that noble characteristic of the Gospel, its native tendency not to wither or to annul the personal being of the Christian but to develope and dilate it to the utmost. I have been reading lately a masterly book, *Some leading Ideas of Hinduism*, by an experienced missionary and highly-trained thinker, the Rev. Henry Haigh. Towards the close of the volume the writer expounds the religious issues of the subtle pantheism of the Brahmins, and elaborately delineates the 'perfect man' of the system, the human person who has worked out, along the prescribed routine of restraint, observation and concentration, his *mukti*, his 'liberation.' What is the condition of the being thus at length set free? He stands disengaged from all relation to other men. To him all persons, all things, all crimes, all virtues, are indifferent. 'He is no man;

26

The Apostle of Christ Jesus

individuality, energy, interest in great causes, self- 2 Tim. i. 1.
sacrificing service for others, these are absent in
him. Sainthood, in the Vedânta, is the dropping
of manhood.'

The Gospel asks of its disciple that he shall
wholly surrender himself to the Eternal, yea, till
he can say, 'I live, yet not I' (Gal. ii. 20). But
then, such is its immeasurable difference from the
ideal of India, it fills the void left by the surrender
of self-will not with *nothing* but with the Lord of
Life and Love. 'Not I—but Christ liveth—*in me.*'
And where He lives, this wonderful, this supreme
Person, 'who loved me, and gave Himself for me,'
there the habitation dilates and unfolds itself
because of the Inhabitant. The ideal Christian is
no passionless vacuum, detached, indifferent. He
is indeed a person still, a person whose whole inner
world of affection, thought and volition is alive as
never before, and in contact more full and tender
than ever otherwise it could be with all around
him. But the centre of the sphere is occupied
now, not by self-love, but by Jesus Christ—
radiating His gracious presence through the whole
sphere of life.

This reflection brings us to the next words in the An Apostle
address of our Letter. 'Paul, *Apostle of Christ
Jesus.*' He had often called himself by that title
before now, in the old days, in the fulness of his
powers and of his ministry. It was his joy then to
realize himself as just this—the Emissary of his
Lord; it filled him continually and at once with a
new quietness and a new energy, animating him for

The Second Epistle to Timothy

'the care of all the Churches' (2 Cor. xi. 28) and for the
thousand common duties and burthens of the day.
It relieved him of all that fatigue which comes of
merely personal ambitions; it precluded the secret
dreariness of self-conceit, the dolorous isolation of
pride, and the corresponding miseries of mortifica-
tion. He belonged to Another; there, in that
settled fact, was involved at once a repose and a
motive inexhaustible. He was the chosen and sent
Emissary of Another; in that thought the whole
work of preaching and of pastorate was dis-
burthened of the haunting sadness of doubt, and of
that exhaustion of the soul which comes with a
continual publicity, and it was filled with a sense
of sure commission and of never-failing support, as
he rested in his Sender's will. And now once more,
yet once more, close to the grave, old and worn-out,
and in the persecutor's final grasp, he calls himself by
the old title and rests with all his weariness upon it.
He is 'Apostle of Christ Jesus,' even to the end. He
can travel no more, and he has done with governing.
He will never found another Church, nor ever plan
another tour of inspection and development. He
has but to bid farewell and to die. Yet he remains
to the last in the unaltered possession of the same
Sender. Even if his message-bearing is reduced to
one last word to the executioner, he remembers with
perfect peace that he is still the Chosen Vessel—
'chosen not for good in him,' yet chosen, and at
the Chooser's service to the close, and then for
ever.

A serene dignity breathes in this final use of the

The Apostle of Christ Jesus

apostolic title. It means an absolute service. It 2 Tim. i. 1. implies, in this man's case, a life which has been full of exhausting and difficult labours, and now a death violent and unjust. But it means also a relation to JESUS CHRIST profound and special; to belong to Him, to be used by Him, in life and in death. And this not only gave a divine energy to the fulness of St. Paul's prime; it infuses here a divine tranquillity into his parting hour.

It is good to live, it is good to die, possessed by Christ Jesus, 'a vessel meet for the MASTER'S use.'

7

CHRIST JESUS

2 Timothy 1: 1

'APOSTLE of Christ Jesus.' Let us look at these
words once again, to take note of the blessed Name
itself, and to ask what it may mean for us as a
spiritual message here.

'Christ Jesus'

'CHRIST JESUS.' Such here is the order of the
two words in the best supported reading of the
Greek. It is an order peculiar to St. Paul, and
very frequent with him. His brethren, Peter, John,
James and Jude, all write always 'Jesus Christ.'
I do not pretend to offer any assured account of the
difference ; but it has long seemed to me, I scarcely
know how, that this Pauline order breathes a certain
feeling of worshipping while intimate *affection* towards the blessed Lord. It may be a precarious
conjecture, but at the worst it lies in the direction
of St. Paul's heart and thought; it adapts itself to
a sense of attachment mingled with adoration on the
one hand and the magnetic force of a consciousness
of infinite obligation to the adored One on the other.
'The Son of God, who loved me, and gave Himself
for me' (Gal. ii. 20): that is the deep melodious
keynote of the whole Pauline presentation of 'Christ
Jesus' to other hearts.

Ubiquity of the Name

Observe again, in these two opening verses of our
Letter, *the recurrence* of this beloved Name. It is
written three times over within these two or three

30

Christ Jesus

lines:—'An apostle of *Christ Jesus*'; 'The promise 2 Tim. i. 1.
of the life which is in *Christ Jesus*'; 'Grace, mercy
and peace, from God the Father and *Christ Jesus*
our Lord.' Here again is a note intensely characteristic of St. Paul; this ubiquity of the Lord throughout his whole thought and writing. But indeed it
is essentially characteristic of the New Testament at
large. Take almost at random any great portion of
the Book, and mark there with a pencil the recurrence of the mentions of Him and of the references to
Him. A certain exception appears in the Epistle of
St. James, where the Name occurs relatively seldom,
though the few mentions are full of weight and
power. But the rule is far otherwise; in a New
Testament so marked the pages will continually be
found starred and scored in every part.

Now to us, with our long familiarity with the Bible Its Signifi-
and the Gospel, this phenomenon may easily fail to cance
look as impressive as it is. Try then to open the
Book with something of the feeling which you would
bring to a new-found document, disinterred by
literary explorers last year from some Egyptian or
Sinaitic concealment, and then read these endless
references to that Name again. Forget for the
moment the particular assertions about this wonderful 'Christ Jesus': does not the mere unwearied
reiteration of His name, taken by itself, bear a
witness as deep as can be borne to His supreme
greatness and glory in the writers' hearts? They
cannot move, they cannot think, they cannot feel,
without Him. He is the beginning and end of their
arguments and appeals. He is the life-blood of their
own spirits. He is the one great secret, the vast

The Second Epistle to Timothy

'unsearchable riches' (Eph. iii. 8), which they are bent upon imparting to others. Upon Him as their redemption, their peace, their security, they rest. By Him, joined to their very being, and living in their hearts, they move. When they look up to the silent heavens, He is there, their Priest, Advocate, King, Friend, Forerunner; 'at the right hand of the majesty on high.' When they look round upon the Church, the believing Congregation, He is there, 'Christ in them, the hope of glory' (Col. i. 27), 'Christ all, and in them all' (Col. iii. 11). When they contemplate Creation, He is its cause and law, its corner-stone, its end (Col. i. 16, 17). When they think themselves into the vast future, He is there, ready to return, 'this same Jesus,' 'appearing without sin unto salvation' (Heb. ix. 28).

In Him they know God. From Him they have the eternal Spirit. And the eternal Spirit's delight is, according to their teaching, to glorify Christ to them, to reveal God's Son in them, to join them to the Lord (Gal. i. 15, 1 Cor. vi. 17).

Even if the Bible contained no express statement that Christ Jesus is GOD, what short of that supreme truth could this inexhaustible abundance of His Name, in the very Book of God, really mean? Everywhere in that Book He is the manifestation of God, the way to God. Yes, and such a manifestation, such a way, that we never get beyond Him, never dispense with Him. HE is 'all our salvation and all our desire,' blessed be His Name. Therefore He must needs be One with Him whom He makes our own.

He was all this to the dying Apostle. He is to be all this for our living selves to-day.

8

'LIFE': 'MERCY'

2 Timothy 1: 1,2

SOME few more phrases of the opening address of the Epistle ask for our reverent notice.

2 Tim. i. 1, 2.

i. St. Paul has announced himself as the 'apostle of Christ Jesus, through the will of God,' that will which marked him, spared him, called him, 'put him into ministry.' And he is this, '*according to* the promise of the life which is in Christ Jesus.' That is to say, his apostleship 'runs on the lines' of that great promise. It was given with a view to it, given in order to carry it out. God, 'by His prophets, in the Holy Scriptures' (Rom. i. 2), had promised of old a wonderful reversal of man's death, his first death and his second death alike, in 'Him that was to come.' Then arrived the promised Prince of Life. And having lived, and died, and risen, He must needs be preached. So, eminently among others, this man, Saul of Tarsus, was transfigured from a blasphemer into a preacher, on purpose that 'the promise of the life' might take effect.

According to the Promise.

ii. '*The life* which is in Christ Jesus.' Here is one out of several great summary designations of the Gospel. We have others of the same order. Sometimes it is 'the Cross'; sometimes 'the Spirit'— notably in 2 Cor. iii. 6, where the word stands in antithetical contrast to the Law, and denotes the

The Life

33

The Second Epistle to Timothy

Gospel as the revelation of our capacity, by the pentecostal Gift, to meet and to do God's will, 'written in our hearts.' And here the Gospel is 'the Life,' a word glorious in its simplicity and its depth, summing up all the wealth of blessings into one radiant thought.

For indeed 'the Life' does thus gather them all up into their end and issue. What is it, ultimately, which was to be given to us through Incarnation, Atonement, Pentecost? It is the Life eternal. It is that wonderful thing, the highest life, which means immeasurably more than even an indestructible existence, for it speaks of the springing and flowing for ever in man of those blissful forces which he was created in God's image to bear and to employ for ever. It means the possession and fruition of what man can be when he is spiritually 'joined to the Lord' (1 Cor. vi. 17); of the eternal Life, when he 'knows' (Joh. xvii. 3), as happy spirits know, 'the only true God and Jesus Christ whom He hath sent.' 'The Life'—this is what it means. Germinating here, bursting from its vernal bud into its summer flower hereafter, it is nothing less than this — man immortally one with God in Christ, moving and rejoicing with His living and life-giving love, seeing Him, knowing Him, and for ever tasting the perfect and royal freedom of 'serving Him day and night,' even as the limb in its pure health finds its strength and pleasure in acting out the purpose of the head.

iii. And this Life is '*in Christ Jesus*' — and nowhere else. He is its sphere, its secret; nay,

34

'Life': 'Mercy'

He is it:—'Christ which is our Life' (Col. iii. 3). 2 Tim.
'He that hath the Son, hath the Life' (1 Joh. v. **1, 2.**
12), and he alone.

Wonderful phrase, as written down here from the
lips of St. Paul! Around the man who thus spoke
of 'the promise of the Life' the last shadows of
the valley of death were closing, and the noise of
that cold Jordan which our mortal nature fears
could be heard through them, near at hand. It
did not matter! This man 'knew the only true
God and Jesus Christ whom He had sent.' So he
could look up from the shades around him and
could see, above him, the living Star of the eternal
morning, 'the LIFE that is in Christ Jesus.' Let
us in our turn, living and dying, recollect that, in
'that same Jesus,' that same life, deathless as the
heaven from whence it comes, is ours. 'He that
liveth and believeth in me shall never die' (Joh.
xi. 26).

iv. 'Grace, *mercy*, peace, from God the Father **Mercy**
and Christ Jesus our Lord.' Here I do not try to
comment on the whole sacred greeting; on 'grace,'
the loving favour of the covenant Lord; on 'peace,'
the sweet fruition of it in the soul; nor on that
Source of both, Twofold yet One, the Father and
the Christ. We only note now the word, embedded
between these more familiar others—'*mercy*.' So
placed, it is peculiar to these two Epistles to
Timothy;[1] it is characteristic of just these last
messages of St. Paul. And is it not significant as
such? The great life is drawing to its end. The

[1] In Tit. i. 4 it should be omitted from the Greek text.

saint looks forward, and sees, without one misgiving, the coming glory (iv. 8). But he also looks back, and sees the infinite forbearance which has dealt with him. And he looks upward, and then inward, with the solemn insight of the dying, and sees more than ever his own unworthiness in the dawning radiance of his Lord. And thus, the nearer he draws to the assured bliss, the more he knows, for himself and his beloved one, and the more he needs must say, that grace and peace, as the gift of God to sinners of the earth, exist only because of an immeasurable *mercy*.

9

A PATHETIC THANKSGIVING

2 Timothy 1: 3,4

I THANK God, whom I serve from my forefathers with pure conscience, that without ceasing I have remembrance of thee in my
prayers night and day; greatly desiring to see thee, being mindful
of thy tears, that I may be filled with joy. A.V.

I give thanks to our God, whom I worship as *my* fathers did
before me with a pure conscience, that I keep unintermitted my
recollection concerning thee in my petitions, by night and by day;
yearning for a sight of thee, (remembering thy tears,) that I may
be filled with joy.

THE initial address of the Letter is over and the 2 Tim. i.
substance of the message now begins. The form 3, 4.
of the beginning is highly characteristic of St. Paul.
Again and again in other days, writing to the
Churches, he had opened his Epistles thus, weaving
together his thanksgiving and his prayer. Now for
the last time, to this greatly loved individual, he
will open so again.

It is a beautiful and pathetic thanksgiving. What His Thanks-
occasions it is the fact that he has Timothy always giving
in his heart, always in his prayers. It is as if he had
felt that in these sorrowful closing days he might have
found himself faltering in the exercise and tender joy
of this sacred friendship, might have had his heart's
sight of Timothy confused and almost lost in the valley
of the shadow of death. So he 'gives thanks to
God' that it is otherwise; he is grateful to the grace

The Second Epistle to Timothy

2 Tim. i.
3, 4.
which keeps his life-worn heart young enough still
to embrace his dear one in the tenacious arms of
prayer. 'By night and by day' Timothy is present
to him before the throne of grace. As the cheerless
days in the deep prison close and open upon him;
as he lies waking in the night; as he sits thinking,
alone or with Luke, when the pale light shines again;
he is constantly telling the Lord about Timothy,
and asking for him mercy, and cheer, and the drying
of his tears, and, if it be possible, that Paul may see
him once again, to the great, the perfect joy of his
aged and yearning heart.

In passing he drops one notable word about his
relations with his God. 'Him I worship, as my
With a Pure fathers did before me, with a pure conscience.'
Conscience Here two points present themselves to our notice.
First, he asserts the purity of his conscience, just
as years before he had done, in even stronger terms
(Acts xxiii. 1), before the unjust High Priest: 'I
have conducted myself as regards God with all good
conscience up to this day.' Are we surprised at
what looks so much like a self-righteous claim in
this great preacher of penitence? Is this really a
contradiction to such words as those of Eph. ii. 3,
where he says that '*we*' (note the self-including
and self-condemning pronoun) 'once lived our life
in the desires of our flesh, doing the willings of our
flesh and of our minds, and were by nature children
of wrath, just like the rest of men'? Not at all.
It is the self-same conscience which here asserts its
purity and there feels its load. Here, to Timothy,
he only affirms that his worship was the worship not

38

A Pathetic Thanksgiving

of the hypocrite but of the devotee; that it was 2 Tim. i.
single-minded in this respect, that he *meant it* to the 3, 4.
uttermost.   There, to the Ephesians, he joins himself
with them as a lost sinner, 'totally depraved,' that
is to say, morally damaged throughout his whole
being.   True, he had bowed his head to his fathers'
God in a devotion perfectly sincere.   Yet none the
less he was then an unsaved sinner still, corrupted,
lost.   He had yet *himself* to discover.   He had yet
to learn to 'fly for refuge' to the God whose majesty
he had owned but whose holiness he had but half
seen, and whose love he had not seen at all.

Yet that 'pure conscience' was not nothing.   It
was indeed no merit.   But it was a great gift of
mercy that he had been true, not false, that he had
meant his adoration.

Then, secondly, so had his 'fathers' done before As did his
him.   Very moving is this backward look towards Fathers
them.   St. Paul came of a line of ancestors
who were sincerely godly according to their light.
Compared with the light in which he now walked
their day was cloudy.   But they too *had meant* their
adoration; and their almost beatified descendant
here clasps that fact with a loyal affection to his
heart, as, with that instinct of retrospect which is
frequently so strong in dying men, he reaches back to
his pious 'fathers' and feels their spiritual oneness
with himself before their God.

It is just so that Latimer bids us think of
our 'fathers,' in the times of shadow before the
Reformation, with thoughts of peace and hope.
For fidelity to God and His truth, even to the fire of

The Second Epistle to Timothy

martyrdom, means in its nature no narrowness of sympathy and no narrowness of hope.

Thus, thinking of his 'fathers,' he expresses now a yet tenderer affection towards his 'dear child.' The 'tears' of Timothy's parting agony start, as it were, in Paul's own eyes. And his own soul is faint with a 'homesick yearning' (the Greek verb means no less) for one more sight of Timothy on the mortal shore. And by night and by day he prays that it yet, even yet, may be.

10

FAITH AS A FAMILY TRADITION

2 Timothy 1: 5

WHEN I call to remembrance the unfeigned faith that is in thee, which dwelt first in thy grandmother Lois and thy mother Eunice; and I am persuaded that in thee also.   A.V.

Getting a reminiscence of the undissembled faith in thee, faith which resided first in thy grandmother Lois and thy mother Eunice; yes, and I am sure that it doth so in thee too.

'THAT I may be filled with joy.'   This was the wish, the 'homesick yearning,' with which he thought of seeing Timothy again; a beautifully human longing, which the surest foreview of the coming heaven and the eternal reunion there did not annul—taking from the eager heart indeed all sadness of despair, but only quickening, deepening, glorifying the wish for another interview *on earth*.   And here we gather that the wish had in it not only the thought of simply seeing that dear face again, but of seeing in it the light of the Lord, the look *of faith*, the solemn brightness which means that the living Christ is indeed (Eph. iii. 17) 'in residence in the heart, by faith.' ^{2 Tim. i. 5.} ^{A Human Longing}

This I take to be the connexion of the words here, where St. Paul calls up the fact that Timothy had indeed *believed*, had received Christ with 'undissembled faith,' a reliance entirely genuine, and that in that faith he had lived to Him and overcome the world.

41

The Second Epistle to Timothy

2 Tim. i.
5.
Faith

This was a very ancient watchword with St. Paul. Who that has entered into the inner heart of his writings can ever long separate in thought St. Paul and Faith? We know what he meant by that well-loved word; no mere credence of the head, a bare mental acquiescence in the proof of historical or dogmatic facts, but far rather the trust, the reliance, of the quickened heart. Faith, in the thought of St. Paul, meant to embrace with empty arms Christ Jesus in His fulness. So that we may describe faith, from the converse point of view, as Christ in His fulness embraced with empty arms. For in the Pauline Gospel faith is no independent saviour, if I may phrase it so; it is no secret *in itself* for our deliverance from wrath, and sin, and death. It 'saves' only in the sense that it receives the saving Christ. And why, we ask, is He to be received just thus, by this mere *reliance* of the heart? Because it is precisely such a reception which gives to Him all the glory and leaves to the recipient absolutely none. Faith is the bare, the empty, palm of the mendicant, who possesses nothing but asks everything. Thus and therefore faith is 'capacious of Christ,' alike for pardon, for holiness, and for heaven.

St. Paul thinks of his 'dear child' as the man of faith, and therefore as the man of Christ. Therefore, and only so, it will be a sacred joy, even on the threshold of eternity, to see his face again.

Holy
Memories

Then, thinking thus, his heart travels back into a dear past, antecedent even to Timothy. Years ago, in a strangely unlikely place, in superstitious and violent Lystra, he had found (Acts xvi. 1) the young

Faith as a Family Tradition

Lystrian believer, whose Jewess mother (her name is 2 Tim. i. 5. given us in this verse only) was already 'a disciple.' And *her* mother, the aged Lois, so here we learn, was a disciple too. They must have been 'in the Lord' for some years already at that date. For Timothy, when Paul called him out to be his missionary-companion, was of course an adult man. But these pious women, the mother and the grandmother, so we safely infer from this same Epistle (iii. 14, 15), had been teaching him the Word of God 'from early childhood.' They were very probably 'original disciples' (see Acts xxi. 16), fruits, more or less directly, of Pentecost itself; later, in the magnetism of grace, they had been drawn to St. Paul and he to them, so that their names were now among the treasures of his heart.

With what manifest tenderness he recalls them here! How their distinctive character as 'believers' possesses him! He does not dilate on their moral beauty, their fine capacity for the friendship and fellowship of the Gospel; there is no necessity that he should do so :

> 'More need not be told than this ;
> They believed in Jesus.'

'Undissembled faith resided in them,' as in a settled home. And thus Christ filled their hearts; for we have seen that such faith means, in practice, *Christ received*. And thus they came to be for ever a part of the Apostle's life; blended into it by the common possession of the one dear Lord.

And their faith, St. Paul is 'sure' of it, 'resided'

likewise in their child; Christ filled him also. To see him, to see them reproduced in him, above all to see their Lord in him, will indeed be joy to his departing spirit.

O beautiful heredity, where the Lord has so blessed the influence of the holy elder life that its very type is repeated in the younger, so that in a certain sense the son has not faith only but *the parent's* faith! So it was with Timothy, so it may be, so it shall be, in the generations of the faithful, even to the end of days.

11

A CALL TO HOLY COURAGE

2 Timothy 1: 6-8

WHEREFORE I put thee in remembrance that thou stir up the gift of God, which is in thee by the putting on of my hands. For God hath not given us the spirit of fear ; but of power, and of love, and of a sound mind. Be not thou therefore ashamed of the testimony of our Lord, nor of me his prisoner : but be thou partaker of the afflictions of the gospel according to the power of God. A.V.

For which reason I remind thee to fan into flame the grace-gift of God which is in thee through the laying-on of my hands. For God did not give us a Spirit of cowardice, but of power, and love, and discipline. So be not thou ashamed of the testimony of our Lord, nor of me His prisoner ; but suffer with the *suffering* Gospel, according to the power of God.

THE Apostle approaches the special needs of his 'dear child.' He has told him of his love, of his tender memory, of his tears, of his 'homesick yearning' for yet another sight of him on earth. But the main purport, the solemn burthen of the Letter, cannot be satisfied thus ; he must come to Timothy's call and his sacred duty, and in view of it he must speak of Timothy's weakness and of his strength. *2 Tim. i. 6-8.*

In our prefatory readings we saw enough of the character of Timothy, as it is sketched for us by narratives and letters, to understand every word here and its special point. St. Paul is writing to a man of the gentlest and most sensitive spirit, one to whom at the best of times difficult duty was a formidable load, and who was now about to suffer a deep bereavement, to face a hostile world alone, and to *Timothy in face of Duty*

The Second Epistle to Timothy

2 Tim. i.
6-8.

try to do his pastoral duty still. Timothy would be tremendously tempted to yield to the 'cowardice' which fails and sinks in prospect of the evil hour. The enemy of his soul, and of his cause, would whisper to his sick heart the hopelessness, the futility, of the struggle. The terrible world would seem indescribably hard to meet without succumbing to the 'shame' attaching to a seemingly lost and certainly hated cause, and to a leader utterly discredited.

His
Ordination

What should he do? Where in his bewilderment should he turn for courage, and for the power to labour on? The Apostle takes a method perfectly practical; he directs him to a concrete fact, an event not only of his inner but of his outward life; he reminds him of the laying of his own hands on Timothy's head and of the spiritual import and issue of that act. We cannot reasonably doubt the exact reference here; it is to Timothy's Ordination to the ministerial office. Turning to the First Epistle (1 Tim. iv. 14) we find a manifestly illustrative passage. There he is similarly reminded of a 'grace-gift,' lodged in him 'through prophecy,' that is to say, through inspired preaching, 'with laying on of the hands of the Eldership,' the representatives of the ministry of the Church. We reasonably assume in the two passages a reference to the same occasion, having regard to the extremely similar contexts, in each of which occurs an appeal to Timothy to use his 'grace-gift' (*charisma*), which is connected, in each instance, with a laying-on of hands. And we gather that the complete account of that memorable

46

A Call to Holy Courage

2 Tim. i.
6-8.

hour was that the Apostle, perhaps at Lystra, perhaps at Ephesus, had called around him a circle of presbyters; that their hands with his had been laid on the young designated pastor, and that a 'prophet' of the Church, perhaps the Apostle himself in his prophesying character, conveyed the eternal Master's message of power to the ordained man's soul, and, it may be, foretold to him 'what great things he should suffer for the Name's sake' and what victories, in the strength of the Spirit, he should win.

If I read that scene at all aright it meant no Its Significance and Power mechanical or as it were magical injection. Rather it was what Richard Hooker says that the holy Sacraments are, a '*moral* instrument of salvation'; it demanded for its efficacy the yielded will, the living faith, *the receiving action*, of Timothy himself. But on the other hand it was no merely emblematical or pictorial performance; it carried with it a real efficacy to the man who really in his soul received what God, through just that 'laying on of hands,' then offered him. Such was that deed to Timothy that for ever afterwards he might say to himself that, in and through that Ordination, he held a perfectly definite guarantee that special spiritual power for special spiritual work was his; his to claim, to draw upon, to use. He possessed the warrant; let daily faith turn it into the current gold of ministerial power.

May Ordination to the ministry of Christ in His Church to-day be, by the man who bears it, ever viewed, and ever used, as St. Paul bade his son in the faith view and use his Ordination then. So the

47

2 Tim. i.
6-8.

ministry will be a ministry of power indeed. It will be no mere discharge of a round of duties, however laborious, however important; it will be the conveyance of a divine influence to men through consecrated man, in whom the Spirit's fire is 'fanned into flame' by faith. 'Power, love, discipline' of self, and a wonderful faculty for disciplining the lives of others for God and holiness, will work in and from such a ministry. It will be lifted above the misery of being 'ashamed of the testimony of our Lord' in a world which ignores Him. It will 'suffer with the suffering Gospel,' in a life of prevailing sacrifice, sustained from within its depths by 'the power of God.'

12

AN ALL-SUFFICIENT REASON

2 Timothy 1: 9,10

WHO hath saved us, and called us with an holy calling, not according to our works, but according to his own purpose and grace, which was given us in Christ Jesus before the world began ; but is now made manifest by the appearing of our Saviou · Jesus Christ, who hath abolished death, and hath brought life and immortality to light through the gospel. A.V.

Who did save us, and did call us with holy calling, not according to our works but according to his own purpose, and to the grace which was given us in Christ Jesus before eternal times *began*, but which was manifested in the event ($\nu\hat{\nu}\nu$) through the appearing of our Saviour Christ Jesus, annulling death *as He did*, and casting light upon life and immortality through the Gospel.

ST. PAUL is still intent upon lifting Timothy's soul aloft to the full courage of faith. To do so to the utmost he here carries him backward and upward, to the deep past of eternal Love, and to that supreme crisis when the Love unveiled itself in the facts of our redemption. Let the troubled and almost broken servant of God, seeing toil, sorrow, and solitude before him, recollect the sovereign grace which had thought of him before the universe began to be. Let him remember that in that most ancient 'covert of the Almighty' the believing Church, and he as one of its members, had been already provided for 'in Christ Jesus,' his Surety and Head. Then let him think on that great stream of historical mercy which had flowed for his salvation from those hidden springs. Let him grasp again the absolute fact that

49

The Second Epistle to Timothy

2 Tim. i.
9, 10.
'Jesus died and rose again,' the Son of the Father's love, the Saviour of the believer's being. Let him reflect that death, which seemed not only to darken but to ruin everything round him, was itself a thing for him 'annulled'; its actual extinction was now secured in Christ. Let him gaze on the now certain glories of a 'life' present already within him and soon to burst into open 'immortality'; remembering that this was now no half-seen thing, dimly visible at best, as in the comparative dusk of the Old Testament revelation; no, it was now 'brought out into the light' (so we may paraphrase the radiant Greek); it was made plain for faith to see, as faith rested on a victorious Saviour, risen again to die no more.

In the power of these supreme truths, while he 'fanned his grace-gift into flame,' Timothy was to walk, even through his valley of tears, like one who already

'Saw as in a vision
The land Elysian,
And in the heavenly City heard
Angelic feet
Fall on the golden flagging of the street.'

How the
Gospel meets
our Needs.
We have a noble illustration here of that characteristic of the Gospel, its power to bring to bear the supreme and inmost truths of eternity upon the most concrete and practical experiences of time. For labours alike and for sorrows, for the things which seem to fill the path of the pilgrimage so often with stones and thorns, not to speak of snares, the Gospel delights to give us this antidote, at once so loving and so sublime, the revealed facts of an eternal Purpose,

the long-prepared and now for ever finished Sacrifice **2 Tim. i.**
and Victory of the very Son of God.   It is content **9, 10.**
with no prosaic secret in which to meet even our
most prosaic needs.   It understands those needs in
all their depressing reality.   But it knows how to
transfigure not only us but them, to sanctify the
pilgrim and also to glorify the pilgrimage, with the
light and with the holy fire of an eternal love, embodied in a SAVIOUR historically risen and now
alive for evermore.

It is moving to see St. Paul thus, in his last **He repeats**
messages, taking up again, one by one, very briefly, **an old**
with little of his old wealth of words but with all **Message**
the certainty of the prophet, the truths which glowed
so brightly as he unrolled them in other days to the
Romans, the Galatians, the Ephesians.   He soars once
more in the mysterious upper light of that Purpose
which willed the salvation of sinners before the first
star, the first nebula, the first film or tremor of what
we call matter, came to be.   He sees there a sovereignty, the sovereignty of love, granting to us sinners,
foreseen in our awful fall, a rescue and a bliss which
indeed was 'not according to our works'; wholly
uncaused by one shadow of meriting will or meriting
act in us ; to be explained only and for ever by the
Love that willed it.   He hears 'the pleasant voice of
the Mighty One' calling, 'with a holy calling,' the
lost sinner to his Lord and Life ; that 'calling' which
means here, as always in the Epistles (see *e.g.* 1 Cor.
i. 23-28), the invitation which does not only reach
the ear but decides, with tenderest magnetism, the
will.   He sees the wonderful store of 'grace suf-

The Second Epistle to Timothy

ficient,' 'given us in Christ Jesus'; lodged for us
in Him (a safe Depository!) and then disclosed,
liberated, conveyed to us, 'through His appearing'
for us here in His great triumph over sin and death,
so that the eternal life itself shines on us, a celestial
sunrise, from His empty sepulchre.

So the aged Apostle, beside his own grave, bids
his beloved one live already 'in the heavenly places'
and beyond the tomb. There, through that same
grace, in our own day of trial, we too will live,
'waiting for the adoption' (Rom. viii. 23).

13

AN UNSHAKEN RELIANCE

2 Timothy 1: 11,12

WHEREUNTO I am appointed a preacher, and an apostle, and a teacher of the Gentiles. For the which cause I also suffer these things : nevertheless I am not ashamed : for I know whom I have believed, and am persuaded that he is able to keep that which I have committed unto him against that day. A.V.

Unto which *Gospel* I was appointed, as herald, and apostle, and teacher ; on which account I am actually suffering these things ; but I am not ashamed *of it*, for I know Him whom I have trusted, and I am sure that He is able to guard my deposit against that day.

THE Apostle has been encouraging his beloved son. 2 Tim. i. He has called on him to live out his commission to 11, 12. labour and to suffer for the Lord, and to remember the wonderful endowment which came to him with that commission, the 'grace-gift' which was in him, nothing less the Master living in the man by the Spirit's power. He has pointed him back to the primal purpose of sovereign love, 'before eternal times, 'and then onward to the 'life and immortality' which the Gospel has 'brought out into the light.'

Now his thought returns for a moment upon A Soliloquy himself, and Timothy listens to his leader's soliloquy, for such almost it is, about his own commission and his own reliance.

'Unto that Gospel,' so as to carry its message and unfold its blessings, 'he was appointed'—on that well-remembered day, so long ago yet so intensely present

The Second Epistle to Timothy

2 Tim. i.
11, 12.

still, when 'THE LORD met him in the way.' Yes, in these last scenes of apparent uttermost defeat he is as sure as ever of that fact; he knows himself to be the King's own messenger, 'herald, apostle, teacher.' True, the enemy has him apparently in a hopeless grasp. But he is the King's undoubted servant, now as much as ever, and he has only to think upon his King to feel misgiving and despondency vanish at the thought. Nay, his very sufferings are an occasion for an even triumphant reliance. For they are due altogether to the Gospel, and the Gospel is nothing less than the infinitely trustworthy JESUS CHRIST revealed.

Not ashamed

'On which account,' for the reason that he is the apostle of the Lamb whom the world hates, 'he suffers these things;' the dungeon, the abandonment, the unjust doom, the awful solitude. He suffers, but he is 'not ashamed of it'; the seeming wreck is not a real one; what looks like a huge miscalculation, enough to turn to utter disgrace the foresight of the man who embarked his all upon it, is not so by any means. That 'shame' which, as the reader knows, is the frequent synonym in Scripture for disappointment is absent from this sufferer's case altogether. And why? Because he 'knows Him whom he has trusted.'

Repose in a Person

In that one consideration, so simple, so entirely adequate and embracing, lies the whole secret of the indescribable quietness and certainty which breathes throughout this dying Letter, even when the writer drops the tears of human grief upon it. He finds his secret of reassurance in no complex reasonings. He

54

An Unshaken Reliance

certainly does not find it in the aspect of circum- 2 Tim. i.
stances.   He takes a clear and steady review of the 11, 12.
whole field of seeming disaster, and then says, with
a grave tranquillity, 'I am not at all disappointed.'
And the reason is—a Person.

'I know HIM.' This he certainly did.   Historically, he knew Him.   This nameless but known
Person was, 'according to the flesh,' Paul's rather
senior Contemporary; a 'brother' of His, one James
(Gal. i. 19), and many others of His personal
followers, had been Paul's intimates.   And he knew
Him spiritually.   Long before this he had sacrificed
everything (Phil. iii. 8, 9) 'to know Him,' to find
Him the actual Friend of his pilgrimage and
Inhabitant of his heart.   His desire had been
achieved; he knew Him, deeply and dearly indeed,
as his Lord, Life, Way, and End.   He knew Him as
the perfect and absolutely satisfying Object of his
worship and his love.   He knew Him as the Bearer
of his sins and as the Conqueror of his death.   He
was filled all through his being with 'the excellency
of the knowledge of Christ Jesus his Lord.'   And so
—what else could he do?—he had '*trusted* Him.'
He had given himself over to Him, to be saved,
ruled, kept, and guided; and he knew that this act
of trust had been met by the all-faithful Lord.   And
if it was so, then all was well, and well for ever.

The sufferer elaborates no fine drawn theory of his He is able
own safety.   It lies just in this: 'HE IS ABLE to
guard my deposit,' to guard myself and my all,
always, all along.   Through life He will guard it,
through death, and 'unto that day,' that unnamed

The Second Epistle to Timothy

2 Tim. i.
11, 12. day when at length he will see his Guardian face to face.

O unfathomable simplicity, O immoveable 'reason of the hope' (1 Pet. iii. 15)!   Behold faith in action. We perceive that it is a reliance, absolute and open-eyed, upon a Person infinitely trustworthy and infinitely willing to be trusted.   And that Person is 'the same yesterday, to-day, and for ever' (Heb. xiii. 8). Reader and friend, He is the same for me, for thee, as He was for the apostolic martyr.

14

FIDELITY TO TRUTH AND TRUST

2 Timothy 1: 13,14

HOLD fast the form of sound words, which thou hast heard of me, in faith and love which is in Christ Jesus. That good thing which was committed unto thee keep, by the Holy Ghost which dwelleth in us. A.V.

Hold to the model of the healthful words which thou heardest from me, in the faith and love which are in Christ Jesus. The good deposit guard, through the Holy Spirit which dwelleth in us.

THUS St. Paul has uttered in Timothy's hearing his **2 Tim. i.** own personal confession of faith. It has come from **13-14.** such a depth of the soul, a depth where only the **Three Things** greatest and most cherished treasures lie, that in the **Unnamed** expression of it he has not needed to define anything. The Person is not named; the 'Deposit' is not described; the 'Day' is not specified. Jesus Christ, and His follower's own immortal being, and the longed-for Return—these are things in the regenerate heart too great, too primary, to need to be denoted in detail.

Now he returns to Timothy's needs and to his duties.

It has been debated what is meant by the 'model **The Model** of healthful words.' To some the phrase has seemed **of Words** to suggest that even at that early date there had arisen an authorized statement of fundamental Christian truths, a summary of the main facts and principles of

57

the Gospel, a veritable 'Apostles' Creed.' It may
be that this was the case; certainly in extremely early
times some such formulated Confession was required
of those about to be baptized. But the phrase here
does not seem to me to point in this direction;
at least not so clearly as to preclude a simpler
exposition. And this I think is to be found in the
view that by 'the model' St. Paul means here
simply the Gospel itself in its grand lines of truth,
the Message of Christ Jesus incarnate, sacrificed,
risen, ascended, reigning, saving, coming; the Revelation of Him whom, 'knowing,' we 'trust,' and are
'not ashamed.' That Gospel was, from one point of
view, a 'model,' *according to which* was to be
developed the teaching of the evangelist and pastor.
All he should say of truth, of duty, of peace, love,
hope, and everlasting life, all the infinite applications
of such sayings to the hearts of his hearers, was to be
on the Gospel model, arranged along the great Gospel
lines, as St. Paul had traced them for him. He, and
they who heard him, would indeed find those lines
'healthful,' fresh with the open air of heaven. It is
the full-orbed Gospel of the Lord Jesus Christ which
alone is thus 'healthful,' in the whole range of
religious systems. In its majestic wholeness of truth
about God, about Christ, about man, about pardon,
holiness, and heaven, the *full* Gospel is the very
opposite of a morbid or overwrought pietism. It is
spiritual health itself, filled with the life-wind of the
Spirit and with the morning sunshine of the Name of
the sacrificed and risen Saviour.

'To' this Gospel Timothy was to 'hold,' 'in faith

and love '—the graces which were to form, so to speak, the element 'in' which he was to live, as he main- tained his hold.   That 'holding' was to be no mere formal orthodoxy, hardening into a spiritual frost; a mere tenacious grasp upon a creed—a true creed, but a creed taken rather as an external thing than as the expression of soul-felt realities.   He was to 'hold to' it '*in faith*,' practically relying in his daily walk on Him whom it set forth.   He was to 'hold to' it '*in love*,' so walking with Him as to find his soul's affections poured into his belief.   And this very ex- perience of faith and of love was to be '*in Christ Jesus*.'   The pulses of the inmost being of the disciple could only beat aright as he was 'joined to the Lord, one spirit.'

2 Tim. i. 13-14.

Holding fast

Then further this Gospel (so I would explain the connexion of ver. 14 with ver. 13) would become to him 'the good deposit,' the noble, the 'beautiful' treasure committed to his keeping to conserve and to pass on intact.   In other words he was to take jealous care that *the full* message of the Lord Jesus, *the whole* truth about His Person, His Glory, His Love, His wonderful Salvation, constituted his message.   And this Timothy not only should do but could do, 'through the Holy Spirit which dwelleth in us.'   For that sacred Revealer and Teacher, doing His covenanted work for the ordained pastor's special needs, would so 'glorify' Christ to him (Joh. xvi. 14), making his own soul apprehend more and yet more of what the Son of God is given to us to be, that his 'guardianship' should be carried on as with the embrace of an adoring love around the treasure which

The Deposit

The Second Epistle to Timothy

he held, and then his transmission of it should be done as with a voice inspired.

O that the Church, that the Ministry, had more truly and more constantly obeyed that precept! What fitful declines, what catastrophes of faith, what distorted growths of opinion, would then have been precluded in poor troubled Christendom! May the heavenly Master awake us anew to believe, to teach, to toil, 'in the faith and love which are in Christ Jesus, through the Holy Spirit which dwelleth in us.'

15
ST PAUL DESERTED
2 Timothy 1: 15

THIS thou knowest, that all they which are in Asia be turned away from me; of whom are Phygellus and Hermogenes.   A.V.

———

Thou knowest this, that all those in Asia turned away from me; among whom are Phygelus and Hermogenes.

WHO Phygelus[1] and Hermogenes were we do not know.   No other mention of either occurs in Scripture or in any early trustworthy quarter outside its pages; we can only suppose that they were men so well known as adherents of St. Paul that their defection was particularly noticeable and painful.   I may remark by the way that this quite passing allusion to individuals by name, without any assignable reference to things or persons otherwise known, is altogether unlike a fabricator's methods; it is a true token of the authenticity of the Epistle.

But these two men were only chief examples of a host of people, all alike in this, that they lived in Asia and that they had deserted St. Paul in his evil hour.   'Asia' is a word which has curiously changed its reference in the course of ages, till it now denotes that vast region of the globe of which 'Asia Minor' is but a district, while the whole embraces Arabia, Persia, India, China, and enormous tracts beside. Under the Roman system 'Asia' was smaller than

2 Tim. i. 15.

Phygelus and Hermogenes

Asia and St. Paul

———

[1] We should spell the name thus, not Phygellus.

The Second Epistle to Timothy

2 Tim. i.
15. even Asia Minor ; it was a narrow province, including
only Lydia, Mysia, Caria and Phrygia. And good
reason can be given for thinking that with St. Paul
here it meant a district narrower still, the country of
Lydia only, precisely the region in which stood the
'seven churches *in Asia*' of the Revelation of St.
John. Its capital was the mighty Ephesus where
St. Paul (Acts xx. 31) had spent three complete years
at the height of his activity, working in the city and
from it as a centre, till St. Luke could say (Acts xix.
10) that 'all they that were in Asia heard the word
of the Lord Jesus, both Jews and Greeks,' and
Demetrius the silversmith could complain (*ibid.* 26)
that 'almost throughout all Asia this Paul hath persuaded and turned away much people, saying that
they be no gods which are made with hands.' Among
his 'friends' there and then (*ibid.* 31) were 'certain
of the chief of Asia,' or more properly 'certain of the
Asiarchs,' a recognized body of magnates, known to
us from other sources as an institution of Asian public
life. Altogether, looking back over only a few years,
some six or seven before this date, we find St. Paul
a very powerful personal influence indeed in the
whole region in question, from Ephesus and the
coast-country up to Colossæ, the little town far inland
in the glen of the river Lycus. As we read the quiet
narrative of the Acts we may easily fail to realize
how great, how phenomenal, his position was, such
a position that the pagan life of the country was
probably affected by it visibly, so that the temples of
the Gods were manifestly less frequented and their
sacrifices and revenues sensibly reduced. The man

St. Paul Deserted

who in his unconverted days seemed just about to 2 Tim. i. 15. prove the national hero of Israel was apparently now about to prove in heathen Lydia a public religious force upon a national scale.

Think then of the tremendous reversal indicated The Desertion in these few words of the dying Letter, 'All those in Asia turned away from me.' He refers evidently to the dreadful crisis when, somewhere in or very near that district, he was seized for transportation to Rome. The deed was done in the midst of the very population which he had lately swayed with such power for Christ; would there not be a strong popular movement to rescue him, or at least would not the people cheer him with open sympathy, and send him away to his trial with the assurance of a general regard of love and honour? Alas, no; 'all those in Asia turned away from him.' It was worth no one's while to be seen in connexion with him now. He was the suspected and dreaded victim of the alarmed State, the defeated leader of a hated and mysterious movement, now encountered by a reign of terror. Nobody stood up for him; he was left alone.

That surely was one of the bitterest hours of the The Pain and the Anodyne Apostle's life of sorrows. His heart was perfectly human; this dying Letter is ample evidence to that effect. He *felt*, at least as much as we should feel, the complex woe of a time when an irresistible tyranny seized him and at the same time a host of former admirers and followers simply washed their hands of him. Only that MASTER who had so fully tasted the same experience, when the tumultuous

The Second Epistle to Timothy

Hosannas had passed, within a few brief days, into
the fierce call to 'crucify Him,' could quite enter into
that grief. But He could do so, and He did. And
meanwhile His heart-stricken servant 'knew Him
whom he had trusted,' and therefore was at rest
about it all. Had he merely followed his own
emotions, or his own calculations, till they ended in
such a collapse, he *must* have failed under the stress of
this tremendous apostasy, the 'turning away from
him' of a whole country full of 'almost Christians.'
But he had followed JESUS, and he was sure of
HIM. His weariness leaned against the Rock of
Ages, and so it became strength, even when his heart
was pierced by the cruel coldness and disloyalty of
the very men for whom he had spent his soul. He
only paused a moment, as we shall see, to breathe a
prayer of love for some of 'those in Asia' and to bid
Timothy be stronger than ever in the Lord.

For the Lord Jesus Christ is anodyne as well as
power to the man who trusts Him altogether.

16

ST PAUL AND ONESIPHORUS

2 Timothy 1: 16-18

THE Lord give mercy unto the house of Onesiphorus ; for he oft refreshed me, and was not ashamed of my chain : But, when he was in Rome, he sought me out very diligently, and found me. The Lord grant unto him that he may find mercy of the Lord in that day : and in how many things he ministered unto me at Ephesus, thou knowest very well. A.V.

May the Lord give mercy to Onesiphorus' family, for frequently he refreshed me, and was not ashamed of my chain ; yes, when he came to Rome he earnestly hunted me out and found me. The Lord give him to find mercy from the Lord in that day. And how many services he did me in Ephesus thou knowest better *than to need me to tell thee.*

WE have here again a reference to a person other- **2 Tim. i.** wise unknown. Nowhere outside this Epistle do we **16-18.** hear of Onesiphorus ; and thus we have another of **Onesiphorus** those isolated allusions, equally particular and unexplained, which are totally unlike the artifices of a fabricator, certainly of such fabricators as were at work in the early days of Christianity.

So far as we can put the hints given us to- **The** gether, the story here indicated would seem to run **probable** somewhat as follows. Among the residents 'in **Story** Asia' who had been greatly attached to St. Paul was one Onesiphorus, head of a family, whose members also, of course, the Apostle knew. When St. Paul was seized and put in chains, and before his captors embarked him for Italy, Onesiphorus had repeatedly visited him, to 'refresh' his spirit, and perhaps also,

The Second Epistle to Timothy

by timely reliefs and comforts, to 'refresh' his body. At that period of crisis and of terror, when all his compatriots turned from the seeming criminal, this man was 'not ashamed' of association with him. Then later, when the Apostle was actually immured at Rome, some cause unspecified brought Onesiphorus thither also, and he resolved to see his holy Friend again. It was no easy task. The days, as we have seen, were different from those when in 'his own hired house' Paul had 'received all who came to him.' It would appear that he was now shut up in some deeper recess of the Roman dungeons, perhaps in the vaults near the Capitol called, with a bad eminence, *Carcer*, 'the Prison'; dark, dripping, miserable; to be entered, if at all, only by the key of a heavy bribe. But however Onesiphorus had found his way, and had cheered his beloved teacher and father by his presence. All this St. Paul recalls with grateful love, and then, looking further back (so I would explain the last clause of ver. 18), he remembers how, at Ephesus, in happier days of old, this same Onesiphorus had done him many an affectionate service. Well, the Ephesian disciple had now come to Rome for a time, while his family, his 'house,' were still at home in Asia; and the Apostle's thoughts travel direct to them in connexion with their father. Were they by possibility tempted to be faithless too? While Onesiphorus at Rome had been so loyal had his family in Asia been sore tempted to cast the Missionary off? He can but pray for 'mercy upon them, for his heart loves them for the sake of their *paterfamilias*. May they be held up; may they in

66

St Paul and Onesiphorus

2 Tim. i. 16-18. any case be spared, and be found at last in Christ. For Onesiphorus himself, a special prayer goes up from the grateful heart of the saint that, 'in that day,' mercy, eternal mercy, the mercy of the Lord's own 'Well done, good and faithful,' may be his happy portion.

Such seems to me a fair explanation of this passage. I take it as referring to a Christian man, either then present in Rome, or recently there, while his family are at Ephesus. I take it to be a prayer for them separately, the man and the family, because they were for the time separated from one another by lands and seas.

Is he prayed for as Departed? It is probably known to my reader that this passage has an importance of its own, in view of the problem of Prayers for the Departed. It is maintained by many that Onesiphorus was dead; that he had visited St. Paul at Rome and soon afterwards had died; and that now St. Paul prays for him that he may find mercy in the great day.

On the grave question whether we should pray for those who have passed from us, I do not pretend to enter here. Such prayers were undoubtedly used fairly early in the history of the Christian Church, certainly before A.D. 200, although for many generations they took only the simplest and vaguest forms, and certainly did not presuppose any purgatorial sufferings in the case of the Christian dead. Yet for even such guarded and reserved prayers, or aspirations, I for one cannot see *distinct* Scriptural warrant —unless it be here. And here, as I have attempted to shew, there is no need at all to assume that

The Second Epistle to Timothy

2 Tim. i.
16-18.

Prayer
for the
Departed

Onesiphorus had died. Separation from his family by a journey quite satisfies the language of the passage.

Let no *unloving* word be said of those Christians who feel their hearts constrained to follow their departed ones with prayer. On the other hand let a caution, reverent and sacred, rest upon our spirits in the whole matter. On any shewing, the Bible is extremely reticent about it. But surely, were such prayer according to God's will, would not the Bible be extremely explicit in its appeals to us to use it? Would it not exhort us, would it not adjure us, to pray for those who are gone before?

Is it not, as a thoughtful child once said, 'a great liberty to take,' to follow them with prayer into the immediate presence of the Lord?[1] Let us pursue them with love, with longing, with hope, with thanksgivings—but with prayer only in this respect, that for them as for ourselves we ever cry and pray, looking upward, looking onward, 'Come, Lord Jesus'; 'that we, with all those who are departed hence in the true faith of Thy holy Name, may have our perfect consummation and bliss in thy eternal and everlasting glory.'

[1] See W. Hay Aitken: *The Divine Ordinance of Prayer*, p. 159.

17

COURAGE AND ACTION

2 Timothy 2: 1,2

THOU therefore, my son, be strong in the grace that is in Christ Jesus. And the things that thou hast heard of me among many witnesses, the same commit thou to faithful men, who shall be able to teach others also.   A.V.

Thou therefore, child of mine, strengthen thyself in the grace which is in Christ Jesus; and the things which thou didst hear from me, aided by the presence (διὰ) of many witnesses, those things hand thou on to the charge (παράθου) of faithful men, such as shall be competent to teach others also.

IN several various forms the Apostle has put before his son, his 'child,' the call to courage and to effort. He has reminded him of a holy home and its examples; he has pointed him to the revealed secrets of eternal grace; he has alluded to his own sufferings, and to the resources which he has found amidst them for his own soul's strength.   Incidentally under this head he has turned to speak of the universal defection of his Asian friends, and again, taking occasion from that thought, he has touched upon the peculiar case of Onesiphorus and his family.   Excepting those last few sentences (i. 16-18), which seem to spring from a purely personal interest, all has led consistently up to the appeal before us here; 'strengthen thyself in the grace which is in Christ Jesus.'

It was precisely Timothy's need, as we have so often seen.   Naturally anxious and sensitive, he had

The Second Epistle to Timothy

now a great grief, a tremendous bereavement, impending over him. His inmost being was conscious of our mortal weakness, unspeakably aware of the fears that can fall upon the lonely soul. Well, just now, now '*therefore*,' he is to 'strengthen himself.'

So we render the Greek verb, with its 'middle voice.' He is to deal *with himself*. His will is to turn inward; he is to say to his own troubled self, 'Why art thou disquieted?' (Psal. xlii. 5); he is to 'take himself in hand' with a view to a victorious strength.

Alas, how shall he do it? Will not such a reflexive action only discover all the more explicitly the inner weakness, the incapacity, the paralysis? Yes indeed it will be so, if the look inward is to be directed upon Timothy's heart taken in itself. But it is to be far otherwise; he is so to look within as to remember 'Christ, dwelling in his heart by faith' (Eph. iii. 17), and then by an active reliance to make use of the indwelling Lord, and so to find himself 'more than conqueror.'

Grace and Christ

'In the grace which is in Christ Jesus'; such was the secret. He was to retreat within those concentric circles, Grace and Christ, two circles which yet are after all but one; for Grace is not a *thing*, separable from Christ, any more than love and will are things separable from the man who loves and wills. Grace *is Christ* in action and in presence. It is '*in Him*,' just as our faculties are 'in' you, and 'in' me. It is after all HIMSELF, as our Secret, our Refuge, our Resource. Timothy in Him, He in Timothy; this was to be the talisman. And St. Paul could recite his own experience for it, from twenty years and more before (2 Cor. xii. 8-10): 'My grace is

Courage and Action

sufficient for thee, for my strength gets its perfection 2 Tim. ii. in weakness. Gladly therefore will I rather exult in I, 2. my weaknesses, that the power of Christ may overshadow me. When I am weak then I am strong.'

'Grace, 'tis a charming sound.' Now, as then, there is an infinite difference between an appeal to nature and an appeal to grace. For us, as for St. Paul and his dear son, the dark hours may come which will only develope into despair the sense of our own inability. But the recollection of our supernatural union with the tender omnipotence of our Head can precisely at such a time transfigure every trial into an occasion for a triumph as great as it is humble.

So Timothy is to 'strengthen himself.' And the **A Practical** strength he shall find is to shew itself (ver. 2), **Issue** amongst other manifestations, in a noble practicality, instinct with hope. He is to restrain his lamentations, for the cause he loves is not a lost cause at all. He is to provide, like a statesman, like a general, *for its future*, its immortal and ever developing permanence. He is to gather his own truest helpers and followers round him, (perhaps in his depression he had almost forgotten their existence,) and then to pass on to them articulately, fully, solemnly, for transmission by them to another generation, pure and unchanged, the Gospel of St. Paul; Christ sacrificed, Christ risen, Christ triumphant, Christ coming. So his strength should be nobly used. And so his strength should grow. For when the worker can lose himself in his blessed work he finds indeed an anodyne and a power.

18

FELLOWSHIP AND ITS POWER

2 Timothy 2: 3

THOU therefore endure hardness, as a good soldier of Jesus Christ. A.V.

Take thy share in suffering hardship, as a true (καλός) soldier of Christ Jesus.

2 Tim. ii. 3.
A revised Reading

WE vary our rendering here, somewhat markedly, from that of the Authorized Version, as the reader will observe. The reason is that the original Greek text, as it is now satisfactorily settled, demands the omission of the word rendered '*therefore*,' and the insertion into the verb of a syllable indicating *participation*. Both changes bring a certain gain. The redundant and not quite pointed repetition of 'therefore' disappears, and a most important element, full of beautiful suggestion, appears instead of it—the element of fellowship, the thought of not merely 'suffering hardship' but suffering it in company, meeting trial, toil, and peril, not alone but side by side.

'Take thy Share'

'Take *thy share in* suffering.' We have already had the very word, in the Greek, above (i. 8), where we paraphrased the clause, '*suffer with* the suffering Gospel.' Here, if we read the context of thought aright, the Apostle means to call Timothy to 'suffer with the suffering' *messenger* of that Gospel, to share the lot of toil and pain with his chief and friend.

72

Fellowship and its Power

A pregnant and noble difference is thus made. 2 Tim. ii. 3.
The bare summons to undergo is one thing; it may
be a hard, a cold appeal, a mere official order
delivered to a military unit. But the call to come
to the leader's side and to partake with him his own
deep experiences of danger and sorrow is a very
different thing. On the one hand it brings home the
inspiring thought of the leader's own large share in
the soldier's lot; his own experience of the conflict,
and of the watch-fire, and of the broken slumber
upon the field. On the other hand it discloses the
leader's heart towards the follower; the captain's
generous thirst for fellowship, his open avowal of the
help to his own courage which his dear subordinate's
partnership will bring.

Even so the CAPTAIN of our salvation cared that Gethsemane
His disciples should share, in some measure, in His
sorrows. 'My soul is exceeding sorrowful; tarry ye
here, and watch with me' (Matt. xxvi. 38); 'Ye
are they which have continued with me in my
temptations' (Luke xxii. 28). And He has sanc-
tioned the thought of the strength and blessing
of fellowship in trial for all His followers of every
age, when He bids His Apostle write (1 Pet. v. 9);
'Resist the devil in the solid strength ($\sigma\tau\epsilon\rho\epsilon oi$) of faith,
knowing that the same sorts of suffering ($\tau\grave{a}$ $a\mathring{v}\tau\grave{a}$ $\tau\hat{\omega}\nu$
$\pi a\theta\eta\mu\acute{a}\tau\omega\nu$) are being carried to their goal ($\mathring{\epsilon}\pi\iota\tau\epsilon$-
$\lambda\epsilon\hat{\iota}\sigma\theta a\iota$) for your brotherhood which is in the world.'

Yes, there is a deep secret of hope and power The Power of remembered Brotherhood
in the fact of such a 'brotherhood,' the inner
brotherhood of grace, and of a circle more intimate
still within it, the brotherhood of *suffering* 'under

The Second Epistle to Timothy

the mighty hand of God.' In the early days of
the English Reformation a notable group of young
student Christians was planted by Wolsey in his
great foundation at Oxford, Cardinal College, now
Christ Church. All of them, unknown to the
founder, were men powerfully influenced by Luther,
and they all fell into inevitable trouble when their
convictions were avowed. Sharers for a time of
a loathsome prison, they discovered there the happiness and strength of fellowship. 'Brothers indeed
we were in those evil days,' wrote one of the sur-
vivors, looking back long afterwards.

Who that has ever in the least degree *suffered*
in the path of obedience does not know something
of what St. Paul means here? '*Take thy share
with me,*' on the field of battle, at the post of
anxious outlook, in the hour of critical counsel.
And there are always those with whom such share may
be taken; there were once seven thousand of them
(1 Kings xix. 18) when Elijah thought he was alone.

Let us make our times of pain, when they come,
times of renewed remembrance of 'our brotherhood
which is in the world,' and of a renewed resolve
to 'take our share.' So shall the spirit of the
'true soldier of Christ Jesus' revive and grow
within us. So we shall be able to think, not with
reluctance but with the alacrity of faith, that if we
are Christ's indeed we are called not to a holiday
but to a campaign; that our tent is pitched upon
a field of battle; that we are not isolated adventurers,
fighting each for his own hand, but soldiers in the
uniform of the King, sharing alike.

19

PARABLES OF EARNEST LIFE

2 Timothy 2: 4-7

No man that warreth entangleth himself with the affairs of *this* life ; that he may please him who hath chosen him to be a soldier. And if a man also strive for masteries, yet is he not crowned, except he strive lawfully. The husbandman that laboureth must be first partaker of the fruits. Consider what I say ; and the Lord give thee understanding in all things. A.V.

No soldier on active service entangleth himself with the businesses of *ordinary* life, that so he may meet the wishes of him who chose him into the force. If again a man contendeth in the games, he doth not get crowned if he do not keep the laws of the contest. The hard-working farmer must be the first to share the fruits. Consider what I say, for the Lord will give thee intelligence in it all.

HERE we find St. Paul engaged with illustrations, 2 Tim. ii. intended to enforce and carry home his appeal. He 4-7. has laid it on Timothy's heart to collect his courage Illustrations for the Christian conflict, to remember that he has to maintain

> 'A soldier's course, from battles won
> To new-commencing strife.'

And now he follows this up with three miniature parables, the first in immediate connexion with the military idea, the others accessory. True follower of the supreme Teacher, he knows the power of such helps to the moral understanding ; he knows that they are not only serviceable for uninstructed minds but useful often to concentrate and to irradiate the most cultivated thought. Let us take his three sketches in succession.

The Second Epistle to Timothy

i. The Soldier. Here we observe that he puts before us not the soldier merely, who may be on furlough, or in stationary quarters, but the soldier on campaign; the Greek word emphasizes this; it means the man on active duty. As such, he allows of course no other interest to compete for one hour with his military calling. Life may in other respects and under other circumstances touch him at many points, but all this is in abeyance when he is on hostile ground and within range of the arms or the enemy. Little would he otherwise 'meet the wishes' of the chief who, in view of some enterprise of special difficulty or importance, had 'chosen him into the force' selected for the duty. And the Christian man, above all the Christian pastor, is to think of himself under this similitude. From some all-important points of view he is always 'on active service,' on an enemy's ground, and chosen into his Commander's expeditionary force. His inmost spirit is to be kept detached from all such 'entanglement in the businesses of ordinary life' as will mean his being this, or that, or the other, *first*, and the Lord's soldier and servant *second*.

It is almost needless to say that this parable cannot, any more than other parables, be pressed mechanically upon its every detail. The Christian in common life not only may do the world's work but is bound, for his Lord's sake, to aim to do it exceptionally well. The Christian husband, or wife, or parent, is to be, in Christ, the most faithful, the most devoted, the most care-taking that can be. The Christian pastor is to keep his heart and thought

76

Parables of Earnest Life

open to manifold interests in human life around him, 2 Tim. ii. 4-7. and he often may, and he sometimes must, to the great gain of his primary labours, direct his faculties and sympathies to matters of enquiry and mental acquisition not primarily sacred. But one and all, and again, above them all, the consecrated minister of God, must remember steadfastly that they are always 'on active service,' and must always be *first* the soldiers of Christ, and *secondly* whatever else they are. To the Christian clergyman the warning here is absolute. Let him, for his soul's sake and for his work's sake, never dare to forget that all real 'entanglement' is fatal.

ii. The Athlete. This was a favourite metaphor **The Athlete** with St. Paul in years long past, and now, close to the end of his own long exercise in the *palæstra* of Christ's service, he comes to it again. Behold the crown, the 'wreath,' of Heaven, the olive, the laurel, of 'the prize of the high calling'! What will it be for Timothy hereafter to receive it, while 'Well done, good and faithful' is spoken by the blessed Arbiter! But the man who would take it at last must have kept the rules, even as the rules were kept for the Olympic contests. He must be true-born—with the new birth. He must have 'trained' in earnest, 'keeping under his body,' 'enduring hardness' for the Lord.

iii. The Farmer. Here Timothy is led by con- **The Farmer** trast to a similitude totally devoid of excitement, remote from all glamour of peril and of applause. The strenuous and prosaic toil of the tiller, his patience under uncertain seasons, his quiet waiting

The Second Epistle to Timothy

through pains for gains, this all is to enter deep into the life of the Lord's servant; ploughing, sowing, tending, and then reaping at last. That supreme quality is here in view, so great in the Gospel scale of virtues—*the patience that goes on !*

And the Master of the field will surely crown it 'in that day' with an everlasting 'joy of harvest.'

20

A CALL TO RECOLLECTION

2 Timothy 2: 8,9

REMEMBER that Jesus Christ of the seed of David was raised from the dead according to my gospel. Wherein I suffer trouble, as an evil doer, even unto bonds; but the word of God is not bound. A.V.

Remember Jesus Christ risen from the dead, of David's seed, according to my Gospel; in which Gospel I am suffering hardship, even to chains, as a malefactor; but the Word of God is not enchained.

IN the passage last before us the Apostle had at the close referred to 'the Lord,' undoubtedly the Lord Jesus, as the living Interpreter of truth to His servant's heart:—'Consider what I say, for the Lord shall give thee intelligence in it all.' Timothy was referred for insight and exposition not to the Church, not to the Apostle, or to the Apostles, but to the divine Master Himself, present, attentive, cognizant of Timothy's individual difficulties and mental needs; able to set truth before him in precisely the right light, from just the right angle, and to make it evidence itself to his whole soul. *2 Tim. ii. 8, 9. The Supreme Interpreter*

Let us note the words ere we quite leave them. Nowhere does St. Paul more distinctly claim, though he does so only indirectly, to be an authentic bearer of inspired oracles. For he claims Christ as the one true Interpreter of the very lines he is writing. Then on the other side, nowhere does he more distinctly *Important Inferences*

The Second Epistle to Timothy

affirm our living Saviour's power and will to be
precisely this, the true Interpreter of His own
Scriptures. May we always bear that assurance
reverently and practically in mind as we open our
Bibles in His presence.

Remember
But now the Apostle turns to this same wonderful Lord for a far other purpose. He points now
not to His present care and grace, as He whispers
truth into the soul through the Word, but to the
everlasting fact, at once historical and spiritual, of
His Cross and Resurrection. St. Paul essays to re-
assure Timothy's heart for his difficult and dreaded
life by one last and highest argument; it is Jesus
Christ, crucified and risen; Jesus Christ the Fulfil-
ment of all the promises, for He was born 'of the
seed of David'; Jesus Christ the substance of all
the Gospel, as He had sent Paul forth to preach it.
'Looking off unto' (Heb. xii. 2) this wonderful
Jesus Christ, will not Timothy 'strengthen himself
in His grace' for whatever shall be *his* cross, in a
bright assurance that he too shall have his resurrection?

Take the words up in this connexion, and think
them over once again.

'Remember Jesus Christ.' What, is there need
for such a precept?

> 'Remember Thee, and all Thy pains,
>   And all Thy love to me;
> Yes, while a breath, a pulse remains,
>   I must remember Thee!'

**There is
Need**
Even so; but it is grace alone that maintains *such*
a remembrance as those sweet lines imply and as

80

A Call to Recollection

this precept of the dying Apostle contemplates. 2 Tim. ii. 8, 9.
Alas, otherwise, amidst the very stress and noise
of religious work it is only too possible *to forget*
Jesus Christ, till the Christian comes altogether to
lose that living basis of faith and spring of love,
the spiritual sight of HIM.

'Remember Jesus Christ risen from the dead.' The Fact of Christ dead and risen
In other words, keep steadily in view the fact of
your Lord, as once slain and now for ever risen;
risen, as the Greek perfect participle implies, with a
resurrection not only achieved but, in its glorious
issue, in His 'indissoluble life,' permanent and
present. Here two mighty truths roll themselves
into one, and both are full of force for Timothy.
First, Jesus Christ was once among 'the dead.'
He did indeed once 'suffer.' Does His servant
shrink from pain, and from the grave ? Does he
dread the seeming defeat of dissolution ? Let him
remember that his LORD was once entombed, a
lifeless corpse in the long white shroud. Then
secondly, does he doubt, in the bewilderment of his
burthened soul, about the glory that is to follow ?
Does the hope of heaven seem to melt into nothing
in his grasp as he faces the dread facts of earth ?
Let him remember that his LORD, once dead, stands
risen beside him, eternally risen—and his Lord for
him is Heaven. Here and now, there and then, the
Risen One, once buried, is his 'rock, his portion for
ever.' Absolutely historical, for He is 'of the seed
of David' and Heir therefore of all the predicted
'mercies,' He is now and for ever, in the secret of
His servant's spirit, the spiritual Reality which

The Second Epistle to Timothy

2 Tim. ii.
8, 9. stands radiant amidst all forms of shadowy fear, alike on this side the dreaded grave and on the other.

Here lies a 'peace, passing all understanding,' for St. Paul. He *knows* that 'his Gospel' is this Risen Saviour's absolute truth. What then matters the Roman dungeon, while that truth, that 'Word of God,' once liberated from the Jewish grave, is free for ever? Paul may be sure of a final liberty and victory along with it—and so may Timothy be sure, and so may we.

21

SUFFERING, ITS END AND MOTIVE

2 Timothy 2: 10-13

THEREFORE I endure all things for the elect's sakes, that they may also obtain the salvation which is in Christ Jesus with eternal glory. *It is* a faithful saying: For if we be dead with him, we shall also live with him: if we suffer, we shall also reign with him: if we deny him, he also will deny us: if we believe not, yet he abideth faithful: he cannot deny himself. A.V.

For this reason I endure everything, on account of the chosen ones, that they also may obtain the salvation which is in Christ Jesus, with eternal glory. Faithful is the saying: For if we shared His death, we shall also share His life; if we endure, we shall also share His reign; if we shall deny Him, He also will deny us; if we are faithless, He abideth faithful, for He cannot deny Himself.

THE thought of suffering *and its fruits* is still the ruling thought of the Apostle; the glorious gains of pains. He is very near the goal now, very near 'the Father's house, where we lay our burthens down.' But this thought only accentuates the note of self-sacrifice, of willingness to suffer, for the sake of fruit-bearing, even to the last step of the journey. *2 Tim. ii. 10-13. The Gains of Pains.*

'For this reason,' the reason that he is the dear-bought servant of a risen and once crucified Saviour, he can 'endure everything,' anything, in 'fellowship with His sufferings.' And that fellowship makes the cause not of Christ only but of His people precious to St. Paul; he will work and suffer to the end 'on account of the chosen ones,' to help them on their way through grace to glory, through Christ on earth to Christ in heaven. It is his *For the Elect's Sake*

83

The Second Epistle to Timothy

Master's will that the safety of the flock should be
largely bound up with the pains, and the pain, of the
man sent to shepherd them. Well then, the man
will present himself, a living sacrifice, on the altar of
that 'sweet, beloved will,' on account of the flock.
If, in order that they may know JESUS, and may at
last be with Him where He is, Paul must struggle,
weep, and die—it shall be done, and done with the
whole heart of the doer poured into the doing.

The Elect

'The elect' here are undoubtedly the Church, the
Congregation of the disciples. But let us not think
that the word loses its mystery and its greatness by
that large reference. The elect are the Church, not any-
how, but as it is contemplated in its essential reality,
as it is true to its eternal idea. From one aspect they
are Christians taken on their profession, assumed to
be all that '*Christian*' means. From another, they
are those whom the Lord knows to be such indeed;
the souls in which the secret of His grace results in
faith, and hope, and holiness indeed. Bright is their
prospect in His plan; it is nothing less than the
'eternal glory' of His presence above; He will love
them, He will keep them, even to the end, even to
that end. Yet none the less, He who prepares the
end prepares also, and also requires, the means. And
among the means is prepared and provided the
suffering life and death of His pastoral servant,
spending and being spent for them.

The Hymn

And now (ver. 11-13), there sounds in St. Paul's
inner ear a solemn chant of pain and of praise, of
trial and glory; a primeval Christian hymn, as we
may confidently take it to be. He evidently quotes,

Suffering, its End and Motive

and does not compose, the heart-moving sentences in their responsive rhythm. We may group them with
four other utterances—all in the Pastoral Epistles
(1 Tim. i. 15, iii. 1, iv. 9; Tit. iii. 8), and all
introduced by the phrase, 'Faithful is the saying'—
as watchwords of the first believers, so worded, most
of them however, as to lend themselves to song. So
regarded they lie before us as examples of those
'spiritual songs' with which in an earlier day St.
Paul had bidden the believers (Eph. v. 19; Col. iii.
16) to cheer one another's faith and hope. Across
the long ages, through the profound silence of the
past, we seem to catch the music as those dear
Christian voices blend in the sacrifice of song. We
can hear them chanting in the upper chamber,
around the Table of the Holy Supper, on the shore
at parting, and sometimes on the last march to
martyrdom. They come to us as voices of the Spirit
through the faithful Church, even as the Epistles
which now enshrine them and authenticate them are
His voices through the apostolic prophet and pastor.

What a song it is, in its holy awe, its conquering
faith and hope! It goes deep to the foundations of
the Gospel, basing all our peace and power upon our
'share in His death.' It affirms the eternal fact
of His life, His indissoluble resurrection-life, as the
secret and strength of the life of His believing
follower. It looks upward and onward to His
everlasting reign in glory, and to the promise that
the sinners He has saved shall actually share that
glory with Him. It recites His own dread words
(Matt. x. 32) to the disciple who denies Him, and

2 Tim. ii. 10-13.

The Message of the Hymn

85

**2 Tim. ii.
10-13.**

reminds the waverer that 'He cannot deny Himself,' cannot unsay His own plighted word, whether of promise or of merciful forewarning. Above all and through all it sings of HIM, and makes of His Name its one divine refrain. 'The faithful saying' is instinct throughout with the Name of JESUS. The man who overcomes, who lives, who reigns at last above, does so as one to whom is *given* the victory—through our Lord Jesus Christ.'

22

THE TRUE PASTOR'S CALL

2 Timothy 2: 14,15

OF these things put them in remembrance, charging them before the Lord that they strive not about words to no profit, *but* to the subverting of the hearers. Study to shew thyself approved unto God, a workman that needeth not to be ashamed, rightly dividing the word of truth. A.V.

Remind men of these things, adjuring them as in the presence of God not to fight over words, to no useful purpose, but so as to involve rather the ruin of the hearers. Be in earnest to present to God yourself, tested and true, a workman unashamed, holding straight onward through the Word of the truth.

THE thought turns now from Timothy's personal ex- 2 Tim. ii. perience and its underlying principles to his influence 14, 15. upon others. Particularly the Apostle has in view here A Message the pastors and preachers whom Timothy is called to to Pastors superintend, to counsel, to encourage. This comes out in one way or another all through the rest of this second chapter, but most explicitly here, in verse 14, where the first thought is directed to the ruinous effects of 'word-fighting' upon '*the hearers.*' We gather hence that the men to be 'reminded of these things,' that is to say, of this great law of the discipline of suffering, were to be men whose function it was to speak to their listening brethren.

Here is an instructive order of topics, suggestive for The Order all time to the ministers of Jesus Christ. The chief of Topics Pastor is first dealt with, as to the state and history of his own soul, his own proficiency in the school of the Cross. Then, and only then, as one who can indeed hand

2 Tim. ii. 14, 15.

on that truth 'through personality,' he is to press a genuine conformity to the Cross upon his brethren in the work. They in their turn are to remember, unweariedly, their 'hearers.' They are to 'believe, to suffer, and to love,'[1] *never for themselves alone*, but largely also for the flock. They are to think, to reason, to teach, to discourse, with the flock deep in their hearts.

The Misery of 'Word-fighting'

'Adjuring them as in the presence of God not to fight over words.' Would that the soul, the spirit, of that appeal had ruled the Church and its pastors from the first; we should see another face upon the world to-day. Let us not misread the thought, as if the Apostle meant that 'words,' from all points of view, are trifles. No, there are positions and moments when a word is of infinite import. 'God,' 'faith,' 'death,' 'life,' these are but words from one aspect, but to use them aright may mean the whole difference between supreme reality and deadly illusion. To own from the soul, *and with the lips*, that Christ is God, 'my Lord and my God,' may be to take sides decisively and for ever with eternal truth and fact against a dream. Yes, but man has a tendency to 'fight over words' when those words stand less for great realities, ultimate and sacred, than for his own favourite opinions, the constructions of his own mind, sometimes rather the creatures of his own wish and will. He sets them up sometimes as idols to be worshipped, sometimes as curiosities to be examined in a microscope, sometimes as objects on which merely to exercise his mental dexterity. And then, as regards

[1] 'To believe, to suffer, to love, was the primitive taste.' Joseph Milner: *History of the Church of Christ*.

The True Pastor's Call

the soul, and the Lord, and the life eternal, they become dead things, white bones upon a field of battle. The strife about them, though connected with religion, can then become as totally irreligious as anything can be. For it may give those 'hearers' the illusion of being religiously interested when all the while 'GOD is not, in all their thoughts.' 2 Tim. ii. 14, 15.

Let us watch ourselves with peculiar attention when we find ourselves drawn into controversies on religion. Then is the time above all others to resolve that our souls shall live behind and above 'words,' in conscious touch with the eternal THINGS.

Meanwhile *for himself* Timothy was to keep close to his divine MASTER, in order that it might be thus with his own soul. He was to 'present to God *himself*' (the word is emphatic in the Greek), to stand ever at his Lord's beck and call, 'tested and true' before His eyes—'good metal' all through, in respect of the single-hearted will to please HIM. He was to be shy of his own notions, and indomitably faithful to 'the Word of the truth,' the precious revelation of Christ Jesus, His work, His love, and His will; 'unashamed' as he looked up to His blessed face, 'and laboured on at His command, and offered all his works to Him.' The Chief Pastor's own Need

He was (rendering literally) to 'cut a straight line through' that Word, even as the ploughman draws his long furrow true across the breadth of the fertile field. In other words, 'the counsel of God,' and the whole of it, is to be his meditation and his message, from the first and to the last, whoever around him may still be 'fighting over words.'

23

AN ALIEN WISDOM

2 Timothy 2: 16-19

But shun profane and vain babblings : for they will increase unto more ungodliness. And their word will eat as doth a canker : of whom is Hymenæus and Philetus ; who concerning the truth have erred, saying that the resurrection is past already ; and overthrow the faith of some. Nevertheless the foundation of God standeth sure, having this seal, The Lord knoweth them that are his. And, Let every one that nameth the name of Christ depart from iniquity. A.V.

But the *current* profane babblings avoid, for they will advance to more and more of impiety ; and their word like a gangrene will eat yet further in. Among these *teachers* are Hymenæus and Philetus, men who in respect of the truth have gone wrong, saying that resurrection has already taken place, and so upset the faith of some. However, the solid foundation of God standeth *ever*, with this seal upon it, 'The Lord knoweth those who are His own,' and, 'Let him depart from iniquity, whoever nameth the name of the Lord.'

2 Tim. ii. 16-19.
A Solemn Encouragement

It is at once most mournful and yet suggestive of a solemn encouragement to read sentences like these, written in that early morning of the Christian day. A man is writing who was actually contemporary, for a good part of his younger life, with the Lord Jesus. And he addresses a friend who also in all likelihood had often talked with those who had walked and companied with the great Redeemer, and could recall His very accent, and describe His features, and recount wonder-works of His which their own eyes had seen. Yet the Householder's field is already thick with tares among the wheat ;

heresy is all abroad; the most patent and outstand- **2 Tim. ii.**
ing teachings of the Master and His messengers are **16-19.**
denied or travestied, right and left. It was a mystery
of iniquity indeed. Yes, but in that trying scene
'grace did more abound'; the suffering truth lived
down the parody in that difficult time; and it can,
and it will, live down still, even to the end, the
parodies or denials of these later days, overcoming
them by its inborn immortality.

Of Hymenæus and Philetus we know practically **Hymenæus**
nothing, except that the Hymenæus of 1 Tim. i. 20 **and Philetus**
is probably one with him we have before us here.
What their 'profane,' secular, unspiritual, 'babblings' were, we can only guess, but the reference
to a 'resurrection past already' helps us in guessing.
It is likely that we have here one of the earliest
allusions to a type of thought known later as
Gnosticism, or *the 'Gnôsis';* the religion of 'Know- **The Gnosis**
ledge' rather than of Faith; a teaching which
claimed to lead its disciple past the common herd
of mere *believers* to a superior and gifted circle who
should *know* the mysteries of being, and who by such
knowing should live emancipated from the slavery of
matter, ranging at liberty in the world of spirit.

More than probably such was the sense in which,
according to this school, 'resurrection had already
taken place.' The initiated soul, immaterial *and
therefore pure,* by the 'knowledge'—not of self, or
sin, or of a holy God, but—of a mystic secret, was
held to have soared aloft out of the bondage of
matter into a transcendental upper air; not to be
partaker there of the bliss of sanctity and love, but—

The Second Epistle to Timothy

2 Tim. ii.
16-19.
to be released from limitations. Some disciples of
the school put their theory into practice by turning
fiercely on the body and punishing it as evil, *because
material*. And too many took the opposite line from
the same point; they let the body go its way in
sensual sin, while the sublime soul, forsooth, enjoyed
its transcendental liberty.

So these 'advanced' thinkers 'advanced to more
and more of impiety,' on principle. So 'their word
did eat yet further in, like a gangrene,' creeping from
limb to limb of the moral being. 'Their God was
their belly, their end was destruction, their glory was
in their shame' (Phil. iii. 19).

Our Need of Warning

Is the beacon-fire of that experience unneeded now?
Never perhaps since Christianity dawned upon the
world was the mental and moral air so thick as
it is to-day with thoughts which claim to 'emancipate' man from the *low level* and the *narrow views*
of the Gospel of the Cross. Philosophies which,
equipped with the newest knowledge of nature, only
go back to pagan types of speculation; dark teachings, mainly conveyed in secret, about unseen powers,
and about a life other than that shewn to us in
Scripture, beyond the veil of death; these things in
a thousand forms are everywhere about us. Let
us draw only the closer to the LORD, as men who
know themselves, and HIM; and let us hold fast
the Word.

The Antidote

So doing, we now, like the faithful then, shall
abide and remain, however far both thought and
morals may drift around us; and so we shall help
others to be steadfast too. We shall experience

92

An Alien Wisdom

something of what it is to be 'known by the Lord 2 Tim. ii. 16-19. as His own,' as only the penitent and believing can experience it. We shall know Him so that our inmost being will 'depart from iniquity,' with a conscience kept sensitive by JESUS, through the SPIRIT, and with a will animated and kept erect by Him. So we shall have the sacred privilege of being 'living stones' in that 'solid foundation of God,' the true Church of the Firstborn. And so many a restless and unhappy spirit will come to learn the secret of purity and peace, and to be built in its turn into the stedfast yet expanding structure of the spiritual temple.

24

THE HOUSE AND ITS VESSELS

2 Timothy 2: 20,21

BUT in a great house there are not only vessels of gold and of silver, but also of wood and of earth; and some to honour, and some to dishonour. If a man therefore purge himself from these, he shall be a vessel unto honour, sanctified, and meet for the master's use, *and* prepared unto every good work. A.V.

But in a great house there are not only vessels of gold and of silver but vessels also of wood and of earthenware, and some for honour and some for dishonour. So if a man cleanseth himself from these *connexions*, he will be a vessel for honour, hallowed, serviceable to the Master, made ready for every good work.

2 Tim. ii. 20, 21.
The Great House

HERE we have an elaborate and pregnant simile or parable. In the words just previous the Apostle has led us to the thought of the Church, and he leads us now that way again. But the two verses shew us the Church under widely different conceptions. The first view presented to us the believing Company as the Lord sees it in its spiritual reality, the true Israel of grace, the Christendom within Christendom. 'The Lord knows' its members as 'His own,' and they do indeed 'depart from iniquity.' Here the Church is presented to us in an aspect which allows the thought of mixture, a scene in which unreality and unfaithfulness lie side by side with holiness and truth. It is the Church from the external point of view, seen as man can tabulate and survey its body. And the solemn recollection is set before us that it is possible, within the Church so considered, to find a Hymenæus

94

The House and its Vessels

as well as a Timothy, and that therefore the truest 2 Tim. ii.
saint, for all his fulness of Church membership in 20, 21.
respect of order and holy ordinance, must with persistent earnestness watch, and pray, and 'examine
himself whether he is in the faith' (2 Cor. xiii. 5).
For a man may be amply within the Church in regard
of visible privileges, and yet only as the 'vessel for
dishonour' is within the house.

Observe the exact lines of the simile. Before us **The Vessels**
is the familiar conception of a large habitation, with
its various articles of furniture and service, and with
its owner, who has of course the use of them. They
are widely miscellaneous in material and in des-
tination. There is the cup of gold or of silver, for
use upon the master's table at high festival. There
is the wooden tub or earthen pail, for the dirty work
of the household. The master uses the one 'for
honour,' for purposes connected with beauty, with
dignity, with refinement. He uses the latter, or his
servants use them for him, 'for dishonour,' for work
best done out of sight, and which tends to make the
vessel itself repellent. The contrast of this with that
is a contrast not of superiority on the one hand and
a humble position on the other, but rather of the far
different and essential distinction between the reput-
able and the degraded.

The tremendous reflection suggested by the simile **For**
is that in the 'great house' of the Church, the **Dishonour**
Church visible and external, there may be, there are,
members, legitimate members as far as human tests
can go, who yet are 'vessels for dishonour.' They
are used, even by the Owner, but it is for purposes

The Second Epistle to Timothy

2 Tim. ii. 20, 21. degrading to themselves. For example, they are taken to be object-lessons of the power of evil, of the deceitfulness of sin, of the awful treachery of man's heart. Such a 'vessel' was a Judas, an Ananias, perhaps a Demas. 'Therefore let him that thinketh he standeth take heed lest he fall' (1 Cor. x. 12).

For Honour   On the other hand there are the 'vessels for honour,' precious in material, used for ends pure and fair by the personal touch of the heavenly Owner. Their size and their particular end may indefinitely vary. One may be the golden pedestal of the lamp of the upper chamber. Another may be the little cup of silver, unadorned by fine device, only true in metal and clean in condition, used to carry a draught of cold water to the passing pilgrim. But they are all alike 'for honour'; all alike are fit for the Owner's eyes and hands, and all are employed for purposes in which He takes delight.

Such vessels, kept by their Lord and Maker's grace true to themselves and to Him, are 'hallowed, serviceable to the Master, made ready for every good work.' Touched by Him at the springs of will and love, the man takes humble care to 'cleanse himself from' part and lot with all thoughts and tendencies which condone sin and minimize the Lord. He 'awakes to righteousness,' and he keeps awake. He renews day by day the surrender and the reliance which are the soul's two arms, clasping the gift of purity and perseverance in Jesus Christ. And lo, the MASTER finds the 'vessel' — large or small, homely or elaborately beautiful — 'hallowed,' 'serviceable,' 'ready' to His sovereign hand.

The House and its Vessels

Lord and Master, make us thus fit ourselves for 2 Tim. ii. 20, 21. that infinitely precious privilege, a state of consecrated readiness for Thy holy use. We are altogether Thine. Enable us as such so to 'cleanse ourselves from' complicity with evil within and without that we, when Thou requirest us for Thy purposes, may be found by Thee *handy* to Thy touch, in the place and in the condition in which Thou canst take us up and employ us in whatever way, on the moment, for Thyself.

25

YOUTHFUL LUSTS

2 Timothy 2: 22

FLEE also youthful lusts : but follow righteousness, faith, charity, peace, with them that call on the Lord out of a pure heart.   A.V.

But the lusts of youth fly from, and pursue righteousness, fidelity, love, and peace with those who call on the Lord out of a pure heart.

2 Tim. ii. 22.
Timothy's Age of Life and its Temptations

TIMOTHY, at the date of the Epistle, was probably about thirty-six or thirty-seven years old.   This was an age advanced enough for high and responsible office; the historical Church allows of episcopal Consecration at even thirty.   But it was an age at which he must have been considerably the junior of many of the 'elders' of Ephesus, the men whom he had now in some measure to lead and to direct.   And this was just such juniority as might tempt him to certain 'lusts'[1]—anything but sensual indeed yet full of spiritual and practical peril— which would be less likely to beset a *senior* leader.   The necessity for just such an assertion of his position as would avoid a dangerous look of slackness and indifference to order might easily glide, and not least in a nature like Timothy's, not of the strongest fibre, into a harsh assertion of himself.   The 'youthful lust' of having his own way, of being 'in evidence,' of posing as the centre of attention—in short, that fatal 'love of having the pre-eminence' which St. John saw in

[1] 'Lust' was a far more inclusive word in old English than it is now, including every sort of strong *tendency*.

98

Youthful Lusts

Demetrius (3 Joh. 9), and which has been so lament- 2 Tim. ii. 22. able a bane in the Church all along, might easily get hold of him little by little. The 'lusts' which show themselves in the short temper, in talk about the man's self, in slowness to recognize the claims of others, in the throwing of life and labour, so to speak, into an attitude, were very possible at his age and in his circumstances. Well, he was to 'fly from' them, as from a mortal peril to his soul and to his mission. There was to be no compromise or parley. In a closer walk with God, that holy secret of a maturity of thought and view which can make the young saint 'understand more than the ancients' (Psal. cxix. 100), he was to find a secure refuge from 'the lusts of youth.'

Meanwhile his soul's energies were to be spent in Pursuit of Holiness following as well as flight; he was to 'pursue' the graces most opposite to the 'lusts,' and to seize them for his own. He was to covet, so as to develope it into a settled habit, the 'righteousness' which scrupulously regards every claim on self from others, which is ready to take sides with others against self, which will rather surrender a personal preference than act in mere self-will. He was to seek and find the spirit of habitual 'fidelity,' that steady, unobtrusive devotion to the smallest duty entrusted to him in the Lord, without which no amount of energy, or even of pious devotion, in Christian labour can ever be quite to the Master's mind. And these good things were to be sought along with holy 'love.' His was not to be a hard and angular rightfulness: no, let it be suffused with the warm sympathies of a heart opened to the hearts of others by the presence within it of Christ

Jesus. And this would specially exhibit itself in a large delight in union and fellowship with all to whom the Name of the Lord was supreme, all who 'called upon Him out of a pure heart'— taking Him in deep simplicity as their Object of adoring invocation and as their Watchword in duty and in suffering. With such as these Timothy was to 'pursue peace.' It was to be his dear aim and quest to join hands with them, and to co-operate with them, and to give them all generous honour. He was to see to it that no 'lusts of youth' on his part spoiled the possibilities of peace; no crude narrowness of spirit, no incapacity to see patiently their points of view on details where there might be difference between them and him. A holy jealousy against spiritual inconsistency, in himself first and then in others, was to be adjusted (as it could be adjusted, in a gracious reality) with a deep desire for a brotherly unity of spirit with all in whom the Lord's image was visible, and to whom His blessed Name was entirely dear.

Is it not a noble and winning ideal, thus set by St. Paul before his comparatively youthful 'son'? It was attainable then; it is attainable now, in Christ, by the Holy Ghost. In the mercy of God may it be more and ever more developed in the men who correspond to Timothy to-day, the junior leaders of our broken Christendom, men called by character or office to any sort of primacy among their fellows, while yet comparatively early in their manhood. Then shall they see, before they fall asleep at the long work's end, a brighter day in the Church of Christ than we have yet enjoyed.

26

THE AVOIDANCE OF STRIFE

2 Timothy 2: 23-26

But foolish and unlearned questions avoid, knowing that they do gender strifes. And the servant of the Lord must not strive; but be gentle unto all men, apt to teach, patient; in meekness instructing those that oppose themselves; if God peradventure will give them repentance to the acknowledging of the truth; and that they may recover themselves out of the snare of the devil, who are taken captive by him at his will. A.V.

But those foolish and unchastened enquiries decline, knowing that they beget fightings; and the Lord's bondservant must not be a fighter, but gentle towards all men, explanatory, forbearing under wrong; in meekness correcting those contentiously disposed, in the hope that God may sometime give them repentance, *leading* to a full knowledge of truth, and that they may wake up *and escape* out of the devil's trap, held willing captives *henceforth* by him *who sets them free* to do His will, *the will of God*.

The closing words of this passage have demanded, as the reader will have seen, a certain paraphrase. As Greek they are not easy, and we are obliged to turn for help in our rendering to the general context and to the probabilities of thought. Upon the whole the grammar favours our referring the 'captivity,' or literally, the 'taking alive,' to the happy surrender of the once - erring soul to the instruction and guidance of 'the Lord's bondservant.' And on many grounds we may be sure that the 'will' spoken of in the last words is the will of God, not that of His and our great enemy.

The Apostle developes here in most interesting detail one main instruction for Timothy's exercise of

2 Tim. ii. 23-26.

The Translation

Unchastened Enquiries

The Second Epistle to Timothy

self-forgetting patience, love, and peace. Around him, 'in the air' of his place and time, were agitated certain 'enquiries,' tempting enough to an unwise curiosity but really far worse than useless; 'unchastened enquiries,' 'undisciplined,' almost 'uneducated' — so the Greek may be rendered. These beyond doubt were attempts by sheer speculation to pierce secrets which only revelation can open; 'enquiries' into such problems as the origin of evil, and the origin of finite being; a type of thought to which we have had allusion already, in ver. 16 of this chapter, and also in the First Epistle (1 Tim. i. 4). Very noteworthy is the Apostle's description of the thing: 'unchastened,' 'undisciplined.' A crude ignorance lay at the heart of such would-be wisdom; ignorance of limits and prohibitive conditions where *data* cannot be other than fragmentary; above all, ignorance of the awful realities of sin, and of the dread holiness of God, and of the consequent urgency of the problem of man's salvation from guilt and from moral slavery. The 'school of thought' in question lacked one supreme Educator within it, the Holy Spirit of God, who convinces the world of sin, and who glorifies Christ to the soul so convinced, and to it alone. His teaching will blunt no intellectual faculty; nay, it will develope the whole mental world. But it will give a wisdom and humility of direction which will 'decline' the alluring, but never satisfying and never sanctifying, 'enquiry.'

How to decline Strife Timothy is to 'decline' taking these problems up as a mere disputant. He may be right to inform

The Avoidance of Strife

himself as to opinion, but he is not to 'fight' the 'enquirers' — in their own arena. For he, 'the Lord's bondservant,' is not a philosopher but a messenger, not a theorist but an ambassador, carrying a commission holy, unalterable, divine. In his relations with alien thought he is bound therefore, most and always, to keep true *in spirit* to his Master. The 'independent thinker' is to find him invariably *dependent* upon a Person who is, for him, absolute Truth and absolute Authority. He is not indeed to make a virtue of ignorance, or a merit of unintelligence. He is to be 'explanatory,' 'apt to teach'; to take care that his holy message is delivered with all the reasonableness of one who has really *learned* at the feet of Christ, and who can sympathize with perplexity, and who understands something of *his own* limitations. But above all he is 'not to be a fighter,' in the sense of loving a mere mental duel for its own sake, or in the yet worse sense of loving his own way and will in the world of thought for his own sake. He is to bring to bear on strange and non-believing theories that influence so sublimely alien to them, the chastened, humbled, beautiful patience of one who forgets himself in his Lord, and in his brother. He is to recollect that there must be *a moral* element somewhere in the rejection of the eternal Love and Redemption, so it be truly presented; that man's mysterious enemy has to do with such a rejection somehow, through that deep influence which the will can exercise upon the intellect. And that element of difficulty will never be rightly handled by the crude combative spirit;

The Second Epistle to Timothy

2 Tim. ii. 23-26. nay, that spirit will only call all the evil out into a blinder prejudice. Rather, the victory must be sought along the lines of love and sympathy, which grace will delight to follow. Then happy shall be the 'bondservant' who sees his once misguided brother 'wake from the fumes' of moral illusion; set free, but instantly again a captive; self-yielded, with a strange new joy, to the hands of his loving emancipator; blessing him, and rejoicing to become with him the ennobled vassal of the will of God.

27

FORMIDABLE SEASONS

2 Timothy 3: 1-5

THIS know also, that in the last days perilous times shall come. For men shall be lovers of their own selves, covetous, boasters, proud, blasphemers, disobedient to parents, unthankful, unholy, without natural affection, truce-breakers, false accusers, incontinent, fierce, despisers of those that are good, traitors, heady, highminded, lovers of pleasures more than lovers of God ; having a form of godliness, but denying the power thereof: from such turn away. A.V.

———

But take notice of this, that in the last days there will set in formidable seasons. For the men of those days will be self-lovers, money-lovers, boasters, overweening, foul-mouthed, unfilial, unthankful, unholy, unforgiving, accusers, abandoned, unapproachable, hostile to good, betrayers, headstrong, blind with self-esteem, pleasure-lovers rather than God-lovers, retaining indeed a theory of godliness but having negatived its power. And from these men—turn away.

IN this dark paragraph the tone of the Apostle changes with a solemn suddenness. He has been speaking of grave errors of both faith and practice, but with the aim upon the whole to prepare Timothy to deal with them in patience and in love. Now he depicts scenes of advanced evil impending in the future, and he enjoins on him, in view of his dealings with 'the men' whom he should encounter then, to find his safety and his duty in isolation. 'From these turn away.' 2 Tim. iii. 1-5. A Stern Paragraph

The passage has its obvious difficulties. To be sure, the lurid account of prevalent evil, evil developed evidently (ver. 5) *within* the Church of What is its Import?

Christ, is illustrated only too largely in many a 'season' of Church history, and under a wide variety of conditions. Often indeed has the thought risen in the mind of the student, the preacher, or the poet, that such is the state of 'Christian' society around him in his own time that the last of the last days must be upon him. So Cowper thought, late in the eighteenth century:

> 'The prophets speak of such, and, noting down
> The features of the last degenerate times,
> Exhibit every lineament of these.'[1]

And he calls on the absent Lord, in a strain of majestic earnestness, to come and 'make an end of sin.' And Cowper's lamentation can be paralleled from a long series of witnesses all down the ages before him. But the suggestion of this passage *might* seem to be that St. Paul is anticipating in the very near future, well within Timothy's lifetime, both a tremendous developement of evil within the Church, and 'the end of the age.' Was it really so? Did the forecast shape itself thus within his soul?

The
Apostolic
Expectation
It is no part of the orthodox creed of inspiration, if I apprehend it aright, to think that the Apostles, as Prophets, could at will map the chronology of the future and say with decision *how long* the Lord would tarry. But on the other hand I fail to see proof in their writings that they definitely expected, as a fact, an early date for His longed-for Return. Among other tokens to the contrary I find an important one in the grave, elaborate,

[1] *The Winter Walk at Noon.*

Formidable Seasons

far-seeing care with which St. Paul concerns himself 2 Tim. iii. 1-5. in one Epistle after another with the order and developement of the Christian Society; not at all as one who was looking for the entire cessation of Institutions, in 'another world,' in an age of direct divine manifestation. In view of such hints of his God-guided thought I cannot think that here he is telling Timothy that the Lord is soon coming, and that the next few years will see the last convulsive efforts of the evil which He alone can annihilate. Rather, by 'the last days' I take him to mean the whole 'Christian age,' shorter or longer, the 'times' between the Departure and the Return, whatever may be that date. As to that period he warns Timothy that it will still produce, in the mystery of sin, 'formidable *seasons*,' not one but many, and that of these one at least is impending now for him. If I may offer the conjecture, he is not so much saying that new and portentous sin will mark the very eve of the Return (though it may well be that it will do so) as that the 'world's old evil,' even within external Christendom, will still, even to the end, have its earthquakes and cyclones, its 'seasons' when, in degrees awfully abnormal, 'iniquity shall abound' and 'love in many shall wax cold.'

Such a time seems to have marked the last days of the great Apostles, the latter decades of the first century. How mysterious a phenomenon is this, how humbling, and withal how full of a solemn cheer, as we read the after-story, continued even till now, of the persistent, patient, restoring, mercies of our God!

107

The Second Epistle to Timothy

2 Tim. iii.
1-5.
Our own
Age

For our own day, grave indeed is the message. Ours beyond question is a period when the bonds of both faith and order are strained to the point of breaking. The sanctities of Society, of Home, of Revelation, are everywhere as if on trial—before revolutionary tribunals. It is a 'formidable season.' But here we have the Bible foreseeing it all, foretelling it all. And that same Bible tells us, with the same voice of calm assurance, that the issue of it all shall be the triumph of our King.

28

COUNTERFEITS OF THE TRUTH

2 Timothy 3: 6-9

FOR of this sort are they which creep into houses, and lead
captive silly women laden with sins, led away with divers lusts,
ever learning, and never able to come to the knowledge of the
truth. Now as Jannes and Jambres withstood Moses, so do these
also resist the truth ; men of corrupt minds, reprobate concerning
the faith. But they shall proceed no further, for their folly shall
be manifest unto all men, as theirs also was. A.V.

For of this sort are the persons who are stealing into the houses,
and taking captive weak women[1] with a heap of sins upon them,
led away by every variety of desire, always learning, and yet so as
never to be able to come to full knowledge of the truth. But just
as Iannes and Iambres withstood Moses so these teachers too
withstand the truth ; men corrupted in mind, reprobate as to their
faith. But they shall not proceed too far, for their folly shall be
conspicuous to all men, just as that of *Moses' opponents* was.

'RETAINING indeed a theory of godliness, but having
negatived its power.' Such, as we saw in our last
reading, was to be one 'feature of the last degenerate
times,' seen in these exponents of degeneracy. It is
a remarkable phrase, and reminds us that the gloomy
picture of ver. 1-5 was not so much meant to present
a world raging against the Church as the Church
awfully wounded by evil from within. 'What are
the great non-Christian religions?' said a friend of
mine in my hearing long ago. And he answered his
own question :—'Judaism, Mahometanism, Brah-
manism, Buddhism and—*unspiritual Christianity.*'

2 Tim. iii.
6-9.
Unspiritual
Christianity

[1] The word 'womanlings' has been suggested to represent the
Greek γυναικάρια.

The Second Epistle to Timothy

There lay a keen point of truth beneath the serious epigram.

The 'theory' of godliness, of Christianity, was, in the cases here in view, superficially retained. Apparently the main lines of belief were still nominally respected. But it was a body without breath, a programme without life—'*unspiritual* Christianity.

A subtle Propaganda   Here the account of this final element in the evils of the 'formidable seasons' is carried into some detail. The Apostle has in his view a definite type of propagandists. They are not loud and obtrusive; there is a certain secretiveness about them. They 'steal into the houses' where there is a possibility of conquests to their cause. Their action is largely directed towards an influence over women. Where they find a restless conscience in woman, a soul whose feminine sensibilities have been invaded by sin, and are now harassed by the miseries of fear, so that the unhappy being, unable to close wholly with the mighty remedy of Christ, afraid to yield itself entirely to HIM, casts wearily about for other anodynes— there is the opportunity. There (so we seem to gather) the visitor plies his religious arts. He suggests his occult solutions of the riddles of sin and sorrow; he promises, possibly at the other end of some path of ascetic ceremonial, an emancipation from the bondage of matter, and a commerce with the world of spirits, and he offers himself as the means and agent—at first on trial, then by degrees as a necessity, till the spiritual despotism is complete.

Ambiguous Language   The opposition to apostolic Christianity is never avowed. The terms of the faith are freely employed;

110

Counterfeits of the Truth

God, Christ, the Holy Spirit, Redemption, Liberty. 2 Tim. iii. 6-9.
The rod of the magician of old, of the *Iannes* or
Iambres—traditional names, perhaps preserved in
documents now long lost ; they are said by Egyptian
experts to represent true Egyptian designations—
looked just like the rod of Aaron, and seemed to
live and to move under the sorcerer's spell in the
same way, and in the same form.   Just so the
whispered message of these their successors in St.
Paul's time sounded strangely like the Gospel, and
therefore it beguiled a host of restless and anchorless
souls, called Christian, and, using for its ends woman's
deep emotional influence, it moved and attracted
a whole section of the Church.   But all the while
it was in diametrical antagonism to the cause of the
Redeemer and the truth.   Its 'sin' was not what the
Lord meant by sin, nor was its 'salvation' His holy
deliverance from the slavery of self-will into the
blissful liberty of a full surrender to a Crucified and
Risen King.   At best all was of the earth, earthly,
the creature of man's dreams, not the gift of God.
And through this avenue it gave access to the very
forces of hell, for it led the soul, along a subtle
curve, to reach even the antipodes of repentance,
grace, and glory.

The Apostle, in his Master's name, assures us that
the evil was to have its limits, and to be put to
shame.   But the hour has not yet come for the final
defeat of such subtle counterfeits of Christ.   So let
us watch, and pray, and keep ourselves always in the
eternal open air and holy morning light of the 'truth
as it is—in JESUS.'

29

THE APOSTLE SPEAKS OF HIMSELF

2 Timothy 3: 10,11

BUT thou hast fully known my doctrine, manner of life, pur
pose, faith, longsuffering, charity, patience, persecutions, afflic
tions, which came unto me at Antioch, at Iconium, at Lystra
what persecutions I endured; but out of them all the Lord
delivered me. A.V.

———

But thou didst follow side by side with my teaching, conduct,
purpose, fidelity, patience, love, endurance, persecutions, sufferings;
things of the kind which happened to me at Antioch, at Iconium,
at Lystra; *so as to know* what kind of persecutions I endured; and
out of them all the Lord rescued me.

2 Tim. iii.
10, 11.
IT is with a certain relief that we reach this paragraph
of the Epistle.   For some time now we have been
detained over the Apostle's description and exposure of
a propaganda of error, wilful or miserably misguided.
We have had to breathe, as it were, the malaria of beliefs
and practices which at their best were a vain substi-
tute for the Gospel and at the worst its deadly opposite.
Now with a confidence and frankness as healthy as it is
holy the saint appeals to Timothy's complete knowledge
of his own life, motives, message, and work, and to
Timothy's resultant reasons for a renewed, a redoubled
reliance on that Gospel which he beheld everywhere
around him denied, travestied, derided, or ignored.

Speech about
Self
It is very much more often a man's duty to be
silent, than to speak, about himself.   A great
Christian of seventy years ago, Simeon of Cambridge,
laid it down as one main rule of his life, *Talk not*

112

The Apostle speaks of Himself

2 Tim. iii. 10, 11.

about thyself. Nothing is more likely to hinder the transmission of our Master's witness through us than lightly to break that rule, and to allow it to be supposed by hearers or by readers that self is a favourite topic with ourselves and occupies a good deal of the thought behind our words. Yet this rule has its excepted cases, when just for once, just for a particular and grave reason, it may be our real duty to speak out, whether about inward experience or outward conduct. It was right for Samuel (1 Sam. xii. 3-5), under critical circumstances, to appeal openly to the people to bear witness that his motives and actions had been true and pure. And it was right for St. Paul, under circumstances exceptional for him, again and yet again to do the same, affirming with a noble emphasis and candour the absolute single-ness of his purposes, the perfect disinterestedness of his deeds. When a man *really is* pure in motive, and when the self-spirit *really is* absent from his work, and that work *really is* so carried on that the self-sacrifice is beyond question, then a positive moral grandeur may attend an unaffected appeal to observers to bear him witness that he is at least what he professes to be. And such an appeal may pass, by a vital and natural connexion, into an appeal to them to respect his message and to put to the test its power for themselves. Rightly made, that is to say, made in the spirit of one whose purity of purpose and action refers itself always to the eternal MASTER and to HIS power on the will, such appeals become a testimony not at all to self but to the Gospel and to the Lord.

So it is here. St. Paul points Timothy back to that

The Second Epistle to Timothy

bright yet often stormy 'Christian spring'[1] of his
when first he joined him as his youthful helper. He
reminds him of those old days of the highland home in
Asia Minor; of his native Lystra and its neighbour
towns, Antioch and Iconium (Acts xvi.); of the wonderful scenes he had witnessed there, the preachings, the
crowds, the glad enthusiasm, the offered worship, the
fierce opposition, the battery and assault, the dreadful
stoning; and he does this not at all that Timothy may
think that Paul is great and good, but that he may grasp
afresh the certainty that Christ is true. For that unique
message, the Gospel of a supernatural redemption
which is at the same time a living rule of love and of
everlasting duty, would powerfully evidence itself by
the force which it put forth in the life and conduct of
its messenger. The converted Pharisee, toiling and
suffering with indomitable gladness for the Messiah
whom he had once persecuted with all his heart,
was then, as he has been ever since, a grand evidence
of Christianity; not by the mere fact that he had
somehow come to preach it, but by the mighty
phenomenon of his preaching it *so*, preaching it as what
was his own inmost life, his own spiritual all in all.

Even thus it has been, in measure, all through the
centuries. God be thanked for every reasoned argument for the faith. But ever and again, until the
Lord's Return, the crowning evidence in proof of
Christianity will be the phenomenon of the veritable
man transformed into the living saint.

> 'Thy name to name, Thyself to own,
>   With voice unfaltering,
> And face as bold and unashamed
>   As in our Christian spring.'—BONAR.

30

PERSECUTION

2 Timothy 3: 12,13

YEA, and all that will live godly in Christ Jesus shall suffer persecution. But evil men and seducers shall wax worse and worse, deceiving and being deceived. A.V.

Aye, and all who will to live a godly life in Christ Jesus will be persecuted. But bad man and impostors will advance ever to the worse, deceiving and being deceived.

FROM his own experiences of trial, and also of divine deliverance, the Apostle turns again to Timothy and the thorny path in front of him. The two verses before us are general in their terms, but we can hardly doubt that they are directed specially to Timothy's needs and intended first and most to animate Timothy's troubled and discouraged heart. To him particularly the general truth was to come home that persecution, in some form and in some measure, must touch the life which is true to the Lord Jesus Christ; this prospect he must personally look in the face, even till his spirit should rise to meet it by a new contact of faith with the blessed Master and His will and power. Then also to Timothy particularly the fact was to come home, with a solemn consolation, that the propagandists of error and delusion around him, whatever might be their success in beguiling unwary and restless souls, were on their way to that tremendous failure which finally awaits all wanderings from God. They were themselves victims as well as leaders, 'deceived'

2 Tim. iii. 12, 13.

The Personal Bearing of the Message

The Second Epistle to Timothy

as well as 'deceiving'; and the ultimate issue of their assertions and their efforts could only be the discovery of their miserable mistake, as the delusion worked itself out to its moral catastrophe. Let the 'man of God,' strong in the consciousness of the holy sanity and truthfulness of his commission, regard them, even in their successes, with almost as much compassion as antagonism. 'Firm on the rock and strong in Christ,' let him take up the day's burthen of persecution, 'just for to-day,' and let him also be patient, 'just for to-day,' over the problem of the successes of the 'deceived deceiver.'

The Permanent Significance

Meanwhile for ourselves the message, in its general terms, has an abiding significance. In our day also, and in some respects singularly in it, there is need of all the recollections which can keep the Christian quiet and hopeful under the trial of the apparent triumph of alien teachings. In the field of religious thought, never more than now, it would seem as if almost any form of aberration from the apostolic Gospel, or of contradiction to it, could get a hearing. 'Many of the disciples go back, and walk no more with' (Joh. vi. 66) the teacher who is so antiquated as to 'know nothing but Jesus Christ, and Him crucified' (1 Cor. ii. 2), so that such a teacher often needs solemnly to reaffirm to himself, not at all in a narrow or 'obscurantist' fashion, but in a deep fidelity, the unalterable truth of Christ, just in order that more persistently, and also more patiently, more kindly, he may keep his footing there and bear his witness thence. Nor seldom will he need particularly to remember those last words of the verses before us—'*being de-*

116

Persecution

ceived.' They will help him to think not less gravely
but more gently, prayerfully, and with desires full of
love, even about those who may seem most active and
most capable in some mission of spiritual delusion.

Then further, the sternly faithful assertion of ver. 12
is a message for us also in our day. Somehow, in some
measure, 'persecution' is still one natural incident of
the fully Christian life. Let no unbalanced words be
said about it. There is indeed another side. 'When
a man's ways please the Lord, He maketh even his
enemies to be at peace with him' (Prov. xvi. 7); a
truth largely illustrated in the Christian biography of
all times. And the principle of our verse here touches
different lives in indefinitely different degrees; no attentive observer can doubt that many and many a
loving and humble disciple, called to lead a quiet life
before the Lord in the 'sequestered vale,' 'serves his
generation' with faithful diligence, and passes at last
to rest, encountering scarcely one perceptible *collision*
on the way. But all this leaves untouched the settled
certainty that there lies an eternal difference, nay an
eternal antithesis, between the ideal of 'the world,'
that is to say of all around us which does not love God,
and the ideal of the man or woman who 'knows Christ,
and the power of His resurrection, and the fellowship of His sufferings' (Phil. iii. 10). And antithetical
ideals, once brought together, must collide. And the
collision, under the present order of things, must mean,
for the disciple, pain. It may be the pain of sword
or of fire. It may be the pain of neglect, reproach,
slander, satire, obstruction. But somehow, and
in some measure, the shock and the stress will come.

117

31

THE POWER OF HOLY MEMORIES

2 Timothy 3: 14,15

Bᴜᴛ continue thou in the things which thou hast learned and hast been assured of, knowing of whom thou hast learned them ; and that from a child thou hast known the holy scriptures, which are able to make thee wise unto salvation through faith which is in Christ Jesus. A.V.

But thou, stay thou in the things which thou didst learn and of which thou wast made sure, knowing from what persons thou didst learn them ; and that from an infant thou hast known the holy writings, those which are able to make thee wise, unto salvation, by means of the faith *which rests* in Christ Jesus.

2 Tim. iii. 14, 15. 'Stand fast' Sᴛ. Pᴀᴜʟ comes here directly and explicitly to his dear son again.   Full of the thought, which we can trace all through the Epistle, of the tremendous 'under-tow' around him — to use a term sadly significant to those who know the perils of our sea-shores—he appeals again to Timothy to keep his foothold on the Rock.   For his soul's life he must do so, and also for the sake of his work and witness.   He is a 'man of God.'   Like the great Angel (Luke i. 19) he is called to 'stand in the presence of God, and to be sent unto' men.   So it is supremely important that he should 'stand' indeed, in his own soul's inmost consciousness, sure of his Lord and of the truth.

Two Mementos With this in view, his friend and father here reminds him of two precious aids to steadfastness. The one is the remembrance of the holy teachers to

The Power of Holy Memories

whom he owed his Christian knowledge. The other 2 Tim. iii. is the recollection of the divine nature and virtue of 14, 15. the holy Book to which they first had led him as to the oracle of God.

Timothy, in a world of religious flux, and in order Life in the to the good of that world, is to 'stay in the things Things which he had learnt, and of which he had been made believed sure.' The phrase is vivid and suggestive. He is not merely to 'hold' them as opinions. Only too often the 'holding of views' means a very poor thing indeed, a mental and spiritual state in which nothing better than a thin thread of sentiment, or a languid conservation of what has become habitual, attaches the man to the belief. He 'holds,' but he is not 'held'; nothing in his opinions *grasps* him with a living force. The imagery here is of a very different sort. The man is to 'stay *in*' his beliefs, or rather 'in' *the things believed.* He is to find his home there, and to be always at home. He is to move and breathe among 'the things' which make up the sphere of his faith. The truths which are his creed concerning God, Christ, sin, salvation, repentance, faith, and 'that blessed hope,' are to be always around him, his inner circle, his immediate atmosphere, nearer than anything else. Then they too shall be *in him ;* the faith and the believer shall be fused, as it were, into one reality.

Now, to help himself thus to 'stay,' he is to Timothy's remember how he won his knowledge and his early Home convictions; he is to reflect that he 'knows from what persons he did learn them.' Here, we cannot doubt it, St. Paul refers in the first instance to

The Second Epistle to Timothy

2 Tim. iii.
14, 15. Timothy's home of old, in that turbulent Lystra
where Lois and Eunice found it yet possible to live
the calm life of faith, and where they taught the
child of their hearts the lore of salvation ; opening to
him the blessed Book, Law, Prophets, Psalms, and
telling him of the LORD in whom now all had been
fulfilled.   We seem safe in this assumption when we
read, almost in one sentence, of 'the persons from
whom he had learnt' and of the *early childhood* in
which he had already begun to know his Bible.
Taking these notices in connexion with the words of
i. 5 above and with our study of that passage,[1] we
are bold to say that the main reference here is to the
dear voices which, in that long vanished home, as
now most probably it was, had gently trained him
into faith.

We need not exclude a reference to other helpers
of his soul.   St. Paul may have also in mind here his
own instructions, given long ago to the young man
he loved so well and used so much.   But the
reference, we cannot mistake it, is mainly to the
earliest days and to the faces and voices of the dear
remembered home.

The Witness
of Holy Per-
sonalities   We have thus before us an appeal to one peculiar
and precious element of Christian evidence, the
witness of holy personalities to the solidity of holy
teaching.   Let us not *misplace* that witness, as if it
was the foundation-stone of faith ; for holiness offers
no absolute guarantee against mistake.   But when,
in the case of the Gospel, we have grasped by the
grace of God the moral glory of its teaching, along

[1] Page 41.

with the historic mass of its fundamental facts, and above them all the Fact of the LORD, then it is a noble help to *the heart*, in its co-operation with thought and conscience, to have seen in the very teachers who led us to Christ the living illustration of that power upon the life which Christ undertakes to exercise. The Lois, the Eunice, beautiful because of HIM, are a breathing testimony to the existence of the CAUSE of that fair Effect.

2 Tim. iii. 14, 15.

32

THE SCRIPTURES

2 Timothy 3: 16,17

ALL scripture *is* given by inspiration of God, and *is* profitable for doctrine, for reproof, for correction, for instruction in righteousness ; that the man of God may be perfect, throughly furnished unto all good works. A.V.

Every Scripture is inspired by God, and is serviceable for teaching, for conviction, for correction, for the training which is in righteousness ; that the man of God may be complete, for every good work completely equipped.

2 Tim. iii. 16, 17. The Holy Writings WE have here a great passage, and we can give it only a brief comment. Let us be as concise as possible in details.

Our last section introduced us to the great theme of the Scriptures. Timothy, from infancy, had known the 'holy writings'; so we have literally rendered. The Apostle puts a certain emphasis in his Greek upon the word '*holy*,' as if to say that there was other and competing literature in the field, perhaps referring to the literature of an occult and mysterious knowledge used by the 'impostors.' Whatever the precise emphasis however the reference here is unmistakable ; it is to the Holy Scriptures, and to the Old Testament of course in chief. Of nothing wider, nothing inferior, would a Paul speak as of the 'writings,' the 'letters,' literature, which distinctively were 'holy.' This most sacred literature was able, he says, as its

The Scriptures

supreme function, to make its reader 'wise,' with a 2 Tim. iii. 16, 17. wisdom bearing upon and issuing in 'salvation.' Yes, it would school him in the deep science of the soul—in the majesty and holiness of God, in His love, in the nothingness of man as His adversary or rival, in the greatness and bliss of man as His creature and willing servant, and in that wonderful redemption, through the Lord of the primeval Promise, which should bring man the rebel back to God as man the child. All this these 'holy writings' would unfold to the soul which had received and believed 'the testimony of Jesus,' and took them up with a 'faith which rested in Him.' For thus they would reveal themselves in their true character. They would prove thus to be the witness of the Father to the Son, in order to unfold man's salvation in the Son, with eternal glory.

So viewed, the holy Writings stand forth, in the Inspired terms of our present section, as one deep Golden Treasury of 'Scriptures,' written oracles, 'inspired by God,' owing their power to His Spirit. The process of His work in their production might be, and it was, inscrutable, and therefore the analysis of that work was impossible. But the result was patent. The breath of God was in each 'Scripture,' as man's breath is in his words, making them to be the vehicle of his thought. The messages of the Bible were the utterance to man of the mind of God. To quote the words of Gregory the Great, Bishop of Rome, who died A.D. 604, the contents of that mysterious Book are 'the heart of God in the words of God.' In the Bible that eternal heart speaks out

The Second Epistle to Timothy

its sacred self, that His children may be 'wise unto salvation,' even the salvation of 'knowing Him, and Jesus Christ whom He hath sent.'

Such was the Book of Books to be to Timothy, when as yet it consisted of the Older Scriptures alone, with only fragments as yet of what were to be the Newer. Such it is to be to us, in that grand completeness which somehow — no man can say precisely how—it attained in the primeval age of the Christian Church, and which shall neither be diminished nor increased till yet once again 'the Redeemer shall come to Zion,' and Himself shall 'tell us all things' (Joh. iv. 25).

The Bible and the Man of God

Such was it to be to Timothy as he was 'the man of God,' 'God's man,' the man commissioned as His minister to live wholly for Him and His work in the souls of others. Such is it to be to 'God's men' now. Without impregnation and inspiration by the Bible there can be no 'complete,' 'completely equipped,' Christian ministry. Our succession may be historically faultless. Our accomplishments may be many, our diligence great, our sacrifice of ease and reputation sincere. But if our heart is not filled with 'the heart of God in the words of God' our words and our works will carry with them a strange disappointment and defect; we shall not be 'complete,' as the agents of His will, 'for teaching, for conviction, for correction,' for that 'training' of souls and lives which moves along the line of His sacred 'righteousness,' 'walking worthy of the Lord' (Col. i. 10).

Then let us betake ourselves afresh to our Bible,

124

The Scriptures

and let us never have done with it. It bears the proof of its own supernaturalness within it; for **16, 17.** while it is a 'Library,' which occupied much more than a millennium in its manifold growth, yet behold —it is a Book! And the world is strewn with proofs, after a thousand criticisms, that this unique Book, manifold and one, is the divine vehicle of supernatural results in human souls. Man of God, Minister of Christ, and all true members of the Lord's Body everywhere, 'read the heart of God in God's own words,' and always be reading it again, on your knees, before the real Author's face.

33

THE PREACHING OF THE WORD

2 Timothy 4: 1,2

I CHARGE thee therefore before God, and the Lord Jesus Christ,
who shall judge the quick and the dead at his appearing and his
kingdom ; preach the word ; be instant in season, out of season ;
reprove, rebuke, exhort with all longsuffering and doctrine. A.V.

I solemnly charge thee, before God, and Christ Jesus, who is
hereafter to judge quick and dead, and *I call to witness* His
appearing and His kingdom [1]—proclaim the Word, devote thyself
to this in and out of season, convince, rebuke, exhort, with all
long-suffering and teaching.

**2 Tim. iv.
1, 2.
Closing
Paragraphs**

THE Letter is approaching its end; a few brief
paragraphs and the dictation will be over and the
sheet of papyrus will be full. But those closing lines
contain a mass of matter of supreme interest, and the
tone throughout is eloquent with the lofty urgency
of the final words of a great message. A strong line
of connexion ties the present passage to the last,
although we have to omit from our text, on good
authority, the '*therefore*' given in the Authorized
Version. St. Paul has been speaking of the Message
of eternal truth, to be delivered by Timothy to his
flock and to be passed on by him to 'faithful men'
for another generation. Lastly he has called his
thoughts particularly to the Scriptures, as the vehicle
to man of the knowledge of the love and will of God,
'holy writings' which, lighted up by 'faith in Christ

[1] My translation of this clause attempts to *explain* the difficult
reading which has the best authority.

The Preaching of the Word

2 Tim. iv. 1, 2.

Jesus,' are found to be full of His Gospel and of His
holiness. Can we doubt that the sentence now before
us has a kindred reference? We are not indeed to
make 'the Word' mean precisely the Bible, no more
and no less; there is a sense in which every true utterance of the message of redemption and holiness, even
to 'the end of the age,' is 'the Word.' But we may
assuredly say, what the primeval Church assuredly
believed, that the Bible is the Word *par excellence.*
For it is the *one authorized record* of the workings
of divine Love in meeting our sin and death, and it
is the only Book on earth which carries upon it, from
end to end, in one way or another, the *imprimatur*
of the Son of God as the authentic revelation of
Himself, and of His Father's mind through Him, and
of 'the glory to be revealed in us' because of Him.
Well then may St. Paul pass from his testimony to
the greatness of the Scriptures to this last appeal to
Timothy to preach 'the Word,' preaching it, like
that 'grave person' whom Christian saw in the
house of the Interpreter, with 'eyes lifted up to
heaven, the best of books in his hand, the law of
truth written upon his lips, and the world behind
his back.'

But now—ponder this urgency of the Apostle's
appeal. What is it which thus lies upon his heart
as he looks death full in the face? What is it over
which he thus recalls the presence of the Father and
the Son, and summons up the prospect of the Coming,
and the Judgement, and the Kingdom? It is—the
preaching, the proclaiming, the telling out by the
Lord's commissioned herald to the world, of 'the

A Call of Supreme Importance

127

The Second Epistle to Timothy

Word.' Upon that proclamation all the man's energies are to be bent, and all the resources of an unweariable 'long-suffering,' in face of prejudice, and opposition, and mistake, are to accompany the 'teaching.' His voice, speaking the message which had first passed through his own heart, is to seize every occasion for this supreme labour; he is to speak for Christ to man 'in and out of season'; that is to say, regardless altogether of his own convenience, and not too anxiously regardful, though doubtless, for his work's sake, not forgetful, of the opportuneness of the moment as to others.

'Preach the Word'; proclaim the Message; place the Lord Christ Jesus, by your words in His name, to the very utmost possible, alongside human sins and human sorrows, while there is time, 'while it is called to-day.'

This, in the Apostle's view, as he stood upon the threshold of eternity, was the thing of all things for Timothy to do. True, he would have other duties; he would have to minister ordinances and to be the administrative leader of the mission-churches. But supremely, he was to 'proclaim the Word'; this before all things was man's great need, and this therefore was the Lord's pastoral servant's highest and incessant task.

A Call to the Christian Ministry to-day

Is it not so to-day? We reverently remember the place and claims, in the life of the Church, of ordinances of worship and of 'governments and helps.' But let the ordained minister of God remember afresh, over this dying Letter of St. Paul, the holy greatness of 'the pulpit,' in the widest significance

128

The Preaching of the Word

of that word. Away with neglect and contempt of 2 Tim. iv. 1, 2. preaching, as if it were a secondary thing and of inferior sanctity. Rightly done, it is the Church's absolutely vital requisite in order to efficiency for her Lord. Therefore we will 'charge' one another, before God and Christ, and looking to the coming end, to 'proclaim the Word.'

34

THE MYTHS AND THE WORD

2 Timothy 4: 3,4

FOR the time will come when they will not endure sound doctrine; but after their own lusts shall they heap to themselves teachers, having itching ears ; and they shall turn away *their* ears from the truth, and shall be turned unto fables.   A.V.

———

For a season shall be when the healthful teaching they will not put up with, but, to gratify their own lusts, will for themselves, as itching in their ears, heap up teachers, and from the truth will turn their ears away, and towards the current myths will turn off.

2 Tim. iv. 3, 4.
A Motive from Difficulties

THIS is indeed a sternly *candid* argument for Timothy's redoubled diligence in preaching. It is delightful when the worker finds himself animated to his work by the thought that 'the fields are white,' and that he is sure to find attention and response, and has a bright prospect of the joy of harvest before long. But such is not the appeal here. The Apostle implores Timothy to preach the Word because a time is hastening on for him when he will find it hard to get anyone to listen to him at all; a 'night is coming' as to opportunities and receptivity. He must be busy with his hearers while he can. There is present still around him, in fair measure, a willingness to listen, worship, and obey; he must use it to the uttermost for the message of Christ, the preaching of pardon, and holiness, and heaven. Not very long yet, and he will find his congregations dwindling, and will learn that

130

The Myths and the Word

many of the disciples are following one or another 2 Tim. iv. 3, 4. of a band of uncommissioned propagandists whom they have invited in to tell them something newer, An Alien Wisdom something more mysterious, something more alluring to curiosity, than the Gospel of the Crucified and the dutiful path of holiness. They will be listening to the 'myths,' nebulous stories and reveries of ' Æons,' of ' Depths ' and of ' Silences,' things pretending to solve the riddle of existence and to emancipate the spirit from its material chain, but not at all tending to make sin hateful, holiness dear, or the Christ of Bethlehem and Calvary glorious. No, *that* message will be neglected, if not actually scouted. It will be put away as a thing belonging to the lower levels of thought; cold, bare, angular ; the seekers of a wisdom worthy of elect human spirits must turn another way than this! Yet all the while that other way will be the 'broad way, which leadeth to destruction ' ; a ' wisdom ' which will stifle the conscience and harden the heart through its flattery of the mind.

Well, Timothy must all the more 'devote The Time is short himself,' while yet he can find hearers, to the divine, unfashionable, man-humbling, Christ-glorifying, ' Word ' — remembering God, and Christ, and the Appearing, and the Kingdom. Through that message the eternal Spirit can and will yet work miracles in men. Aye, and even when it shall seem as if the whole world has gone after the pseudo-Gospel, and the days for winning a hearing may be thought to be over, still let him 'devote himself' to the delivery of his Master's message.

**2 Tim. iv.
3, 4.
The
Apostles'
Trial of
Faith** not only 'in' but 'out of season.' Some will still be listening; more will listen than he knows; and a brighter day will even yet dawn again.

We may well pause here, as we have done at many another point in our Epistle, and restate to ourselves the fact, so humbling on one side, so strangely encouraging on the other, of those tremendous disappointments which beset the last days of the Apostles. The trial to their faith and hope must have been altogether peculiar. For they had not, as we have, a long Christian history behind them, full of illustrations of the self-recovering power of the Gospel and of the immortal vitality of the living heart of the Church. They, or however some of them, were permitted indeed, in a guarded measure, to 'dip into the future' with a supernatural foresight, and to catch glimpses of triumphs further on. But this would never quite annul the dead pressure upon their perfectly human hearts inflicted by the awful 'unfavourable events' immediately around them. Ultimately, it would be by faith, and by faith alone, that they would overcome, and 'rejoice in hope.' They would have to fall back in the last resort not on their feelings but on their Lord, known, trusted, taken at His word, felt and followed in the dark.

Then let us in our day, remembering them, 'gird up the loins of our mind' (1 Pet. i. 13), 'and hope to the end,' and carry on to the end the torch of the Word. A very great many people in our later Christendom will not 'put up with the healthful teaching,' 'the word of the Cross,' 'the word of

The Myths and the Word

faith.' Let us see to it that we present that Word 2 Tim. iv.
with intelligence, with sympathy, with a wisdom 3, 4.
caught from the Lord Himself. But let us still
present *it*. And let the faith of a dying Paul
re-animate our hope, our reliance, and our witness.
For that Word, and that Word alone, is still the one
'*healthful* teaching,' instinct with the eternal life.
The future of the miracles of grace lies not with 'the
myths' but altogether with 'the Word.'

35

THE FAREWELL APPEAL

2 Timothy 4: 5,6

BUT watch thou in all things, endure afflictions, do the work of an evangelist, make full proof of thy ministry. For I am now ready to be offered. A.V.

But thou, be sober in all things, endure hardship, do an evangelist's work, fully discharge thy ministry. For I am already being poured out *upon the altar* as a drink-offering.

2 Tim. iv. 5, 6.
St. Paul's Impending Removal

HERE again we have an argument for Timothy's devotion and diligence drawn not from sunshine but from shadow. St. Paul has just charged him to preach the Word because dark days were coming in the Church. Now he tells him to rise up afresh to suffer and to labour because he, Paul, was just about to be 'taken from the head' of his dear Timothy. He was 'being poured upon the altar' of martyr-death; he was 'being *libated*'; his life-blood was so soon to be shed that it might be said to be already flowing, like the wine of libation dropped upon the sacrifice.

This vivid image is an echo from the thoughts of long years before. In that happier first captivity, in the 'hired house,' he had written just so to the Philippians (Phil. iv. 17); 'Yea, even if I am being poured out as a drink-offering upon the sacrifice and the service of your faith, I joy, and I rejoice with you.'

But the metaphor here after all meant for Timothy

134

no poetic picture but just this tremendous fact, that
St. Paul was soon to die, and he to be left orphaned
of that wonderful companionship. In earlier chapters
we have noticed once and again how often this dying
Letter utters or implies that thought; how we feel
it to be wet here and there with the tears of a mortal
farewell, tears shed by the writer as his heart feels
the tears of the receiver. And be sure that this
profound *sympathy* is not absent here; St. Paul
knows here as elsewhere the anguish which his
death will mean for his son. But here the tender
thought passes upward at once into the heroic, or
let us rather say, for it is more Christian to say so,
into the believing, into the devoted. St. Paul is now
in act to be 'poured out'; therefore let Timothy
arise, as if he had never done it before, to 'be
sober,' and to accept suffering with all his heart,
and to labour in the Gospel to the end.

*2 Tim. iv.
5, 6.*

*'Therefore
arise'*

It is the holy logic, conclusive to the believing
heart, which JEHOVAH Himself used so very long
before with Joshua (Josh. i. 2); 'Moses my servant
is dead; *now therefore* arise, go over this Jordan.'
The Master was about to 'bury his workman,' but
He would be present as ever to 'carry on His work.'
And He had need of Timothy that He might do it.
And to do it, let us be sure, would be for Timothy
not only the clearest duty but the most effectual and
benignant balm.

Now, what is the command to him which this
argument from death and loss is intended to enforce ?
Look at it word by word; and if my reader is a
commissioned minister of Christ, let him look at

*Four
Parting
Watch-
words*

The Second Epistle to Timothy

it with a special scrutiny. First, 'be sober in all things':—the Greek points directly to that 'sobriety' which is the opposite to the fumes and bewilderment of the drunkard. Not the so-called sobriety which often means a timid refusal to give the will and energies wholly over to God, the *point-de-zéle* of the worldling, but rather the sobriety which means a soul fully awake, deliberately conscious of eternal realities, 'looking at the things which are not seen' (2 Cor. iv. 18), 'seeing Him which is invisible' (Heb. xi. 27), and accordingly alive to the life which his bond-servant must live, 'yielded unto God.' Then, secondly, 'endure hardship'; do not be the carpet-knight who never really sacrifices and suffers. For such a Lord, and for the dear souls for which He died, be willing to lead a life which daily dies to self-indulgence and to that self-protection which, whether for spirit or for body, shuns exhaustion, or pain, or sorrow, as 'strange things happening to you.' Then, further, 'do an evangelist's work'; remember that you are called not to be the mere theorist of a system however true, or the mere guardian and celebrator of ordinances however sacred, but the evangelist, the message-bearer of the blessed Christ to living (and dying) human hearts; the man who for himself 'knows whom he has believed,' and so has an immediate and absolute certainty that HE is the *Evangelium*, the Good Tidings, for all who want Him and who find Him, and longs to bring them and Him together, loving Him and them. Lastly, 'fully discharge thy ministry'; let it so fill thy life that thy life may all serve to fill it fully out, that 'all thy studies may be drawn that 2 Tim. iv. 5, 6. way,' and that all men may see that thou, O man of God, O man of Christ, hast only one ruling passion, only one master aim, even to 'glorify Him on the earth and to finish the work which He gave thee to do' (Joh. xvii. 4).

36

TWO ASPECTS OF CHRISTIAN DEATH

2 Timothy 4: 6

For I am now ready to be offered, and the time of my departure is at hand. A.V.

For I am already being poured out *upon the altar* as a drink-offering, and the season of my departure is upon me.

2 Tim. iv. 6.

Christian Death

We have already, in our last study, glanced at the first of these two clauses, mainly with a view to its place in the argument to Timothy's heart: '*for* I am already being poured out.' Let us devote the present chapter directly to it, along with the complementary clause which follows. Let us think of these words about Christian death spoken by this great Christian close to his end. They have much to say not for an apostolic martyr only but for us also, the rank and file of what is yet, down to its least notable genuine member, 'one army of the living God.'

The Libation

i. 'I am being poured out as a drink-offering.' Such to St. Paul was his impending death. For him, to be sure, the phrase had a dread particular fitness; when his death came it would come by the sword; the red torrent would flow, like the wine of the altar bowl, drenching the holocaust, enriching the sacrificial fume. But we need not bind the whole truth of the phrase to such a solemn literalism. Every devoted life, if it is really devoted, a word which means so much more than

138

Two Aspects of Christian Death

devout, is a sacrifice offered on the altar of love 2 Tim. iv.
to the God of our salvation, 'a living sacrifice,' 6.
as St. Paul long before (Rom. xii. 1) had called
it. And when that life, devoted to the last, reaches
its climax in a death full of surrender to the will
of God, the blood may not literally be shed, yet
spiritually the death is none the less a libation which
enriches all the antecedent toil and pain. John
sinking to sleep on his bed at Ephesus as truly
'poured himself out' as Paul did when he knelt to
die at the Three Fountains outside the gate of Rome.
Bede, lying down after his life's long work in his
cloister-school at Jarrow, 'poured himself out' as
truly, though in a far different way, as Hus did in
the fire at Constance. To all these saints life was
'a living sacrifice' *even unto death.* So their death,
their last outpouring of the vital power, yielded up
to their God, was the libation upon the sacrifice.

May it be ours, through our Master's grace, so to
be faithful *even unto the libation.* May we, in Him,
'yield to the Lord with simple heart' not only our
full energies but also 'ourselves, our souls and
'bodies,' when they are weak and worn with mortal
exercise. We adore His will; and that will *may*
ordain that they should be 'yielded' to Him rather
as passive under pain or paralysis than as working
on still, in some measure, in their decline. But however, by His grace, 'the spirit shall be willing' to
maintain its happy surrender even to the last, even
till we 'are being poured out.'

ii. Then we have here another aspect of the death of The
the servant of the Lord : 'the season of my departure Unmooring

The Second Epistle to Timothy

is upon me.' The word rendered 'departure,' *analŭsis*, is the Greek original of our 'analysis.' An analysis means a setting free, a detachment, a separation of things or thoughts from one another. The original noun here, like the kindred verb in Phil. i. 23, denotes the undoing of a connexion, as it were the untying of a cord, the weighing of an anchor, so as to set the voyager free to seek the further shore. To the Philippians, in that earlier day, St. Paul had owned that his 'desire' was 'to unmoor, and to be with Christ' (Phil. i. 23). And here the desire is about to become fact; 'the season of his unmooring is upon him.'

'Crossing the Bar'   It was no light thing, we may be sure, when this realization of that desire 'came' actually on.' It is nature, not sin, to shrink from death *as death*. The greatest saints, in their Lord's own words (Joh. xxi. 20), when they come to die, are 'carried *whither they would not*'; they are living men, *embodied* spirits; they would rather 'not be unclothed, but clothed upon' (2 Cor. v. 4). But then there is the glorious other side, which filled St. Paul when he wrote Phil. i. 23, and which surely rose in conquering greatness before him now. The death which in one aspect was a last sacrifice was, in another, that delightful moment when the friendly flood heaves beneath the freed keel, and the prow is set straight and finally towards the shore of HOME, and the Pilot stands on board, at length 'seen face to face.' And lo, as He takes the helm, 'immediately the ship is at the land whither they go' (Joh. vi. 21).

37

A THREEFOLD RETROSPECT

2 Timothy 4: 7

I HAVE fought a good fight, I have finished *my* course, I have kept the faith. A.V.

The good contest I have wrestled out, the race I have finished, the faith I have kept.

Two metaphors, under which St. Paul pictures his life's end, have just passed before us, the libation shed upon the altar, the boat unmoored from our mortal shore, set free to cross the narrow strait of death to the better land.   Here he is metaphorical again, and the metaphors cover now not the end but the course, not martyrdom in prospect but life in retrospect.   And here again, as in the previous verse, the old saint's mind goes back upon mental pictures dear in earlier days, and he sees again the struggling limbs and the swift feet of the Greek athletes.   Life had long ago seemed to him to be vividly parabled by those scenes.   In one great passage (1 Cor. ix. 24-27) he had developed the illustration in minute and powerful detail ; the stern discipline of training, the strict rules, the rejection which must follow an infraction, the straight eager course of the runners, the terribly purposeful blows of the boxers, the wreath of leaves, 'corruptible' shadow of the amaranthine crown of the victorious Christian.   Again and again in other less conspicuous passages (one of them met

2 Tim. iv. 7.

A Life's Retrospect in Metaphor

141

The Second Epistle to Timothy

us above, ii. 5) he had used those familiar and
eloquent associations to animate himself and his
disciples to live true to the Lord, true to present
grace and to coming glory. Once more here, yet once
more, the *athlete of Christ* speaks the old dialect, but
now with the accent of achievement and repose. He
is so very near the end, so very much of the peculiar
trial of his lot is for ever over, the 'journeyings often,'
'the care of all the Churches' (2 Cor. xi. 26, 28), and
so certain is his Master to love him and to uphold
him over those few difficult paces before the end, that
he speaks as if already off the field. Christ Jesus

Anticipation
had enabled him so long for such a life that it was a
relatively minor thing (may we not dare to say it?) to
be sure that He would enable him, with a glorious
adequacy, for the one last step of death.

For such an anticipation of the end St. Paul had
one supreme precedent. His Lord had spoken just
so, as if all was over, when yet for HIM remained
Gethsemane and Calvary; and *they* formed no mere
final incident of His blessed work but the awful
essence of it! Yet He could say to His Father,
in that High Priestly Prayer (Joh. xvii. 4) so full
of love, of peace, of heaven; 'I have glorified Thee
upon the earth; I have finished the work which
Thou gavest me to do.' Only some twenty hours
more, and the anticipation would be supreme reality;
'Jesus said, *It is finished;* and He bowed His head
and gave up the ghost' (Joh. xix. 30).

So thinks and so speaks now His follower, who
has striven so long and run so far in the power of
the grace of the Crucified and Risen. He *looks back*

142

A Threefold Retrospect

already, with the consciousness of a soul half in 2 Tim. iv. 7. heaven, upon the 'good contest,' the 'grand wrestling'; so almost we may render. It is nearly 'wrestled out' now; and the running is just ending at the goal. Yes, all that, practically, is completed and put aside. The days and nights of care and toil, the fight with temptations outward and inward, the conflicts with subtle and aggressive error, 'the thorn in the flesh, the messenger of Satan' (2 Cor. xii. 7), the extreme physical exhaustion amidst the personal perils and half-deaths of those long travellings—it is a finished story. The *palæstra*, the *stadium*—he trained for them rigorously, and he has trodden them long; now he seems to contemplate them as one seated on some green overlooking hill. He has 'kept the faith'; he has been true to the truth of the blessed Name; and that Name is to bring him now no more fighting, no more for ever, only rest, rest for ever with the Lord.

O Christian worker, Christian soldier, Christian pilgrim, in the midst of your 'contest' and your Respice Finem 'running' to-day, or in what *seems* the midst of it, for the end may all the while be just upon you, take heart often from the thought that even so for you, if you are true to the blessed Name, it shall one day be. The last care will have been felt—and cast upon the Lord, the last exhausting effort will have been made, the last witness under difficulties borne, the last sorrow faced and entered, the last word written, the last word spoken. And then the one remaining thing will be to let the Lord, 'the Man at the Gate,' lift thee in, and give thee rest.

38

THE WREATH OF VICTORY

2 Timothy 4: 8

HENCEFORTH there is laid up for me a crown of righteousness, which the Lord, the righteous judge, shall give me at that day. A.V.

There *only* awaits me now the victor-wreath of righteousness, which the Lord shall award me in that day, He, the righteous Judge.

2 Tim. iv. 8.

The Final Hope

WE have lingered a little over St. Paul's metaphorical setting of his work and of its approaching end, and have seen how the forms of thought of his prime recur to him with a profound naturalness as he comes to die. We see him now using the like imagery for that sequel of glory which lies before him, certain with the certainty of the promise of his Lord, beyond the shades of death.

Action and Friction

He has let his heart settle for a moment upon the deep and simple thought of the mere cessation of the long stress, the close of the wrestling, the goal of the race. This is absolutely true to the human nature which is God's own making, and which divine grace, so far from annulling, only deepens and developes. We are so constituted by our Creator that while indeed we are designed essentially for action we can never be ultimately well off under friction. And the metaphors of wrestling and of racing connote not action merely but friction. When once the period of friction in our being reaches its end, if that end is legitimately reached, reached by

144

The Wreath of Victory

one who has 'kept the faith,' loyal to his Master's 2 Tim. iv. 8. word and will, then the reposeful happiness of the soul in the relief, the cessation, the exemption, is a The Bliss of Rest feeling perfectly pure and right. It means no weariness under the will of God, but a thankfulness, deep as the being, that the time has come for doing that will for ever in an action out of which the wear and tear are gone. So it is no sin when the man is 'glad that he is quiet' (Psal. cvii. 30), safe in the 'desired haven.' One after another Bunyan's pilgrims, as they pass the river, rejoicing in their Lord, rejoice in their rest. Valiant will no more need his sword, that 'true Jerusalem blade.' Standfast's 'toilsome days are over.' They rest, and it is good.

But then the Christian's prospect is never merely Yet Rest is not all rest. As we have seen, it is rest in an activity out of which wear and tear are gone,

'*L'éternel mouvement dans l'éternel repos.*'

And it is more than even this. It is a prospect which, for the true wrestler, and runner, and keeper of the faith, includes *a crown*, a 'wreath of victory.'

The brilliant sequel of the Greek's athletic triumph The Wreath and its Glory was his wreath. To be sure, it was only a circlet of 'corruptible' leaves. But what did it not denote and convey to the recipient? A wealth of admiring and generous welcome, above all at his exultant home. Many a little town in those days of old Hellas took down a piece of its white wall in order that its son, crowned with the crown of the Isthmus or of Olympia, might enter it *by a gate unused before!* Loving honour, no mere negative exemption from toil and struggle, was the issue of the physical stress and strife.

The Second Epistle to Timothy

2 Tim. iv. 8. So it was with the Apostle, not merely as he was an Apostle—we shall see more of this in our next chapter — but as he was a faithful servant of his King. He was about to rest, at once, profoundly, gloriously, and for ever, with Him whom he knew and loved. But 'in that day' he was also to receive 'the victor-wreath (*stephanos*) of righteousness' from the hands of the righteous Arbiter of the conflict and of the course. He was to be decorated, to be acclaimed, to be honoured with the open approbation of his Lord.

Grace and Personality All was of course 'of grace.' Had it not been for free grace this man would never have been a believer, a worker, a witness at all. But when grace came it made—not an automaton but—PAUL to be, in all his large personal freedom and spontaneity, all these wonderful things. Its result was—*a person*, responding to the personal will of God, in holy love and self-forgetting sacrifice.

Love crowning Love To that result, in the sublime 'righteousness' which is implied in God's fidelity to Himself, He *must needs* respond in turn with His own 'well done, good and faithful servant' (Matt. xxv. 21, 23), hailing the man 'into his Master's joy.'

Such was the prospect, full of a sinless personal exultation, for this great Christian. Rest, a 'glorious rest,' awaited him now, at once. Then, a little later, 'in that day,' the hand of eternal Love would be extended from the throne, and the LORD would crown with light and power for ever His true servant's love.

39

'NOT TO ME ONLY'

2 Timothy 4: 8

AND not to me only, but unto all them also that love his appearing. A.V.

_____

Aye, and not only to me, but also to all who have set their love on His Appearing.

IT is recorded in the history of the later stages of the European Reformation, about the year 1627, when the papal and imperial authorities co-operated with tremendous severity to extirpate the Evangelical confessors in the Austrian dominions, that a Bohemian nobleman, Wenceslaus of Budowa, was brought to execution for his faith. Before he laid down his head for the sword the Jesuit ecclesiastics made a last effort to win him back to the Roman obedience. He raised his eyes and said, as he put the intruders aside, 'I have finished my course; henceforth there is laid up for me a crown of righteousness.' 'Ah,' responded the fathers, 'those words were true for the Apostle, not for thee.' 'Nay,' he rejoined, 'you forget what follows; _Not to me only, but unto all them also that love His appearing._'

It was a noble application of the profound general principle given in the words here before us. We noticed in our last chapter that the Apostle looked onward to his rest and to his crown not as an Apostle but as a Christian, that is to say as _a man_ who had,

2 Tim. iv. 8.

A Martyr's Commentary

147

The Second Epistle to Timothy

2 Tim. iv. 8. by grace, lived out the fact that he was the Lord's. He was about to taste the peace of the heavenly Paradise and, on another and yet more radiant day, to receive the crown of glory, not because he had filled a supreme pastoral office—for Iscariot was an Apostle; nor because he had been inspired to see into the unseen and the future—for Balaam was a Prophet; but because he had been a true member of the Christ of God. Therefore for every other member of that Head the like bright prospect stood assured. It was assured for Wenceslaus of Budowa, found faithful to the end. It is assured for you, dear reader, and—let me dare to write the words—for me, found simply, in the grace of God, faithful to the end.

Gradations in Glory

Not for a moment are we to infer that you and I, or even a death-suffering Wenceslaus, will receive a crown, a victor-wreath, indistinguishable from that of a St. Paul. The deepest reason of things witnesses surely for differences of greatness and glory in the final bliss. And our Lord's parable, with its 'five cities' and its 'ten' (Luke xix. 17, 19), looks the same way. When the endless heaven and its conditions open at last to the view of the Blessed, they will assuredly find there not only the richest and largest variety as regards personal individuality, celestial *character* in infinitely varied developements; they will find gradations too. Angels have gradation, and find it no limit to their bliss; and the glorified human saints will not be the less 'equal to the angels' (Luke xx. 36) for having greater and smaller in their happy ranks; orders and degrees, carrying into eternity the varying impress of the preparatory life of time. Most true; yet also all such differences will be

148

toned and harmonized all the while into one glorious 2 Tim. iv. 8. *community* by their equal relation to their one beloved LORD. The pre-requisite to every crown will have Yet Community also been pardon and life in Him, love to Him, service for His dear sake. Paul, Wenceslaus, you, I, so you and I in the grace of God attain 'that world,' as by His grace we dare to say we will, are to be as different as possible in other respects before the throne; but all the glorified will be alike in this—that they are there because Christ redeemed and saved them, because they gave themselves to Him, because they are all related to Him for ever. Those planetary fires will indeed 'differ in glory.' But they will all eternally drink in the effulgence of their Sun, and move around HIM in one concentric everlasting life.

Beautifully distinctive is the special note of Love of His Appearing relation to Christ which St. Paul gives us here: 'Not only to me but also to all who have set their love' (so I interpret the Greek *perfect* participle) 'on His Appearing.' At the root of the matter, their love has been 'set upon' Himself. They are conditioned as saints by their having found in JESUS 'all their salvation and all their desire' (2 Sam. xxiii. 5); by a personal satisfaction in HIM, by a personal surrender, in that deep love, to HIM. But this comes out upon the radiant surface in the form of the 'love of His Appearing.' For that 'Appearing' brings with it the *summum bonum* of all their love of Him and joy in Him. It means not only that they, the Bride, will see the Bridegroom as He is, but that HE will taste His own supreme gladness, 'as the Bridegroom rejoiceth over the Bride' (Isai. lxii. 5).

40

A SIGH AND A LONGING

2 Timothy 4: 9,10

Do thy diligence to come shortly unto me : for Demas hath forsaken me, having loved this present world, and is departed unto Thessalonica ; Crescens to Galatia, Titus unto Dalmatia. A.V.

Do thy best to come to me quickly ; for Demas hath left me in the lurch, loving this present life, and hath gone away to Thessalonica. Crescens *hath left* for Galatia, Titus for Dalmatia.

2 Tim. iv. 9, 10. WE pass at this point into a new paragraph of the Epistle and more immediately approach the close. From the contemplation of his blissful future the old Apostle returns to the persons and things of his surroundings. He has still abundant suggestion and message for our hearts, but along a different line.

A Group of Names The paragraph is full of names, and three of them are grouped within these two verses. Of these three Demas and Titus have met us in earlier Epistles, Demas in Colossians (iv. 14) and Philemon (24), Titus repeatedly, and in important connexions, in 2 Corinthians (*e.g.* vii. 6, 13, 14, viii. 6, 16, 23) and in Galatians (ii. 1, 3). Crescens is a new name. All three appear here as friends and followers who have lately left St. Paul, and one, Demas, as having left him under the saddest circumstances, drawn or driven away by 'love of this present life' (*aiôn*) ; that is to say apparently by a preference of temporal to eternal interests, by a sheer dread of sacrificing

A Sigh and a Longing

liberty and life for the unseen things. If I interpret the words aright, Demas was not what Bunyan takes him to have been, in that dark episode of the silver mine at the hill of Lucre; a covetous man, set upon making a fortune, a Balaam, hankering to his soul's ruin after a house full of silver and gold. Rather he was a man smitten with cowardice in that reign of terror; he went away to Thessalonica (where surely he would find warmer and truer disciples than himself, to put him to shame and perhaps to save him) simply to be out of the way of the dungeon and the scaffold. Of the reasons why Crescens, and why Titus, went away we know nothing, and it is impossible not to ask whether St. Paul, however faintly, does not *sigh* over them also. But assuredly he does not group them definitely with Demas; the structure of the sentences deprecates that thought. And the Corinthian Epistle seems to put Titus before us as so distinctly strong and true a Christian and missionary that we are at least *loth* to think that his withdrawal here had any unworthy motive behind it.

We lay the three names aside with the single further remark that they offer, standing as they do here, one of the numberless internal evidences to the genuineness of the Epistle. We may confidently say that no old-world fabricator would have written down such names at all with just so much incident about them—*and no more*. The inimitable note of fact and of nature is in the words.

But now, whatever has occasioned these three The removals, the three men are gone, and the human Apostle's Sigh

The Second Epistle to Timothy

heart of this loving and love-asking being, St. Paul, feels the absences profoundly. The broken circle lets in upon his tired and wounded heart something of 'the cold of space,' the dread pain of solitude.

Is it inconsistent that he should feel thus, and should betray his sadness with the sigh which we almost hear uttered from the page? Has he not just written glorious words about the finished course and the coming crown? What does it matter that he should be left a little lonelier than usual, for a short final hour, just outside the door of Home? Ah, it is the old story of the manifold heart of man, never for one moment denaturalized by grace. He who sighs does yet victoriously believe; and the believer, because he is true man, does yet sigh. Christ the Lord is with him, and he is about to be face to face with Christ. But he misses the familiar mortal faces; and ah, he sorrows over a friend's unfaithfulness to both Christ and him.

Above all, in that warm and yearning humanity of his, he longs for his dearest Timothy. The dawning of the heavenly rest still leaves him intensely anxious to see that beloved face once more. They will be together with the Lord, ere very long. Nevertheless, 'do thy best to come to me quickly,' here in Rome, here on earth, here in the body.

We shall never know for certain whether Timothy came, and came in time. And for long ages of bliss now Paul and he have been together. But the pleading call stands here immortal on the Scripture page, to witness to the place of the human heart in the life of faith.

41

MARK AND LUKE

2 Timothy 4: 11,12

ONLY Luke is with me. Take Mark, and bring him with thee: for he is profitable to me for the ministry. And Tychicus have I sent to Ephesus. A.V.

Lucas alone is with me: Marcus take up and bring with thee, for I find him serviceable for ministration. But Tychicus I am sending to Ephesus.

WE are still in the midst of allusions to persons and their movements, and another *trio* of names is before us. All these three are known to us as associates of St. Paul. Tychicus is first mentioned in the Acts (Acts xx. 4); an Asian by birth, St Paul's companion on his third missionary journey to Jerusalem. In the Apostle's first Roman imprisonment Tychicus was with him, 'a beloved brother and faithful minister' (Eph. vi. 21). Now in these darker days he has been again at his side, and is here specified— if I interpret aright the Greek verb rendered, '*I am sending*'[1]—as the friend whom St. Paul has just desired to travel to Ephesus, to Timothy, and no doubt to take this Letter with him thither.

The interest of the mention here of Marcus, Mark, is great and peculiar. We cannot reasonably doubt

2 Tim. iv.
II, I2.
Three Friends

Marcus

---

[1] It is in the aorist, and so should be strictly rendered, '*I did send.*' But the letter-writer of St Paul's day mentally anticipated the time of the letter's arrival and wrote as if looking back from it to the past. We write as from the time of action. Thus the English *present* here best represents the Greek aorist.

The Second Epistle to Timothy

that he is the Marcus of Col. iv. 10, one of those followers who were a 'comfort' to the imprisoned Apostle at that time, a cheer amidst his cares aad sorrows by their faithful love. It is equally safe to suppose that he is the Marcus of Acts xii. 12, the 'John Mark' to whose mother's door St. Peter went after his mysterious release, to find the disciples praying together for his deliverance. If so, he was the man whom Paul and Barnabas took with them (Acts xii. 25), first to Antioch and then on their earliest missionary enterprise in Asia Minor (Acts xiii. 5, 13), and who so sorely grieved and disappointed St. Paul by turning back and leaving his leaders at Perga, for some not quite worthy motive (Acts xv. 39), the defection which led later to the 'sharp dissension' between St. Paul and Mark's cousin St. Barnabas, and to their unhappy separation. That was a sorrowful and ominous incident. How easily it might have prompted to St. Paul's mind a hopeless application to Mark of the Lord's words about the ploughman who turns back, and have even led him to put down Mark as 'reprobate silver'! Is it not all the more beautiful, and all the more encouraging, to see this very man more than restored —to the Apostle, and to the Lord Jesus? It may have been the loving Barnabas, with whom (Acts xv. 39) he 'sailed to Cyprus,' who helped him back to courage and to sacrifice; for assuredly Barnabas, however hotly he had 'dissented' from Paul, was still *himself*, and would long all the more to see his cousin wholly right with God because he had been, perhaps, his too eager advocate with man. But,

however, so it was. Marcus, a few years after his 2 Tim. iv.
spiritual defeat, appears as St. Paul's 'comfort.' 11, 12.
And now, a few years later again, in the very reign
of terror, he is so 'serviceable for ministration,' so
capable, so active, so devoted, so sure to be ready to
come and help, even in formidable Rome, that he
must be 'taken up and brought' with Timothy.

Such in outline was the story of this man 'of like
passions with ourselves'; this Evangelist, this
writer (for such he was) of our wonderful oldest
Gospel, yet also this poor frail man, more than
restored by the loving power of God. Shall not his
experience of self, and of grace, cheer us about
others now? Shall it not cheer us about ourselves?

Lastly we come, reading backwards, to that dear Lucas
name, Lucas, Lucanus, Luke. Him too we have
met before. In the Acts he does not write down his
own name. But in those large and vivid sections of
the Acts which run in the first person, beginning
with xvi. 10 (where 'we' gathered that the vision
of the man of Macedonia was the call of God to
'us') we see him as at once the author of the
memorable narrative and the fellow-traveller of
St. Paul. Then again in Colossians (iv. 14) and
Philemon (24) he is with him in the Roman
lodging; 'the physician,' 'the beloved physician.'
And now, behold, the stern testing time is come, and
fair-weather friends fly away to right and left. But
Luke is there, upon the spot; 'Lucas alone is with me';
not indeed the only true friend left to him in Rome,
for he will presently be sending Timothy greetings
from other loyal hearts before he closes (ver. 21), but

The Second Epistle to Timothy

2 Tim. iv.
11, 12. apparently the only one who resolutely stays at his side in the dolorous prison, making it, for that dear leader's sake, his home.

St. Luke is a beautiful and noble example of a phenomenon most congenial to the Gospel. His own writings seem to disclose him to us as a man thoughtful, cultured, mentally gifted, the perfect antithesis to the militant zealot. He was, for his day, the man of science, trained to a refined profession. He was master of a style which has a distinction of its own. He was a true historian by nature. But also, by grace, he was the temple of the possessing Spirit. And in that power the instructed and accomplished man was found, in the midst of the Neronian terror, quietly heroic at his post of love.

42

THE CLOAK AND THE BOOKS

2 Timothy 4: 13

THE cloke that I left at Troas with Carpus, when thou comest,
bring *with thee*, and the books, *but* especially the parchments. A.V.

The cloak which I left behind at Troas, at Carpus' house, bring
when thou comest, and the books, particularly the parchments.

WHAT a prosaic message, what a matter-of-fact com- 2 Tim. iv.
mission! Such may be the reader's first reflection; he 13.
may almost wonder that Holy Scripture has room for A Matter
such details. But the God of Scripture has room in of Detail
His heart for every detail of human life; and human life
is mainly written in prose, and in detail, and is matter
certainly of fact. Poor and shallow is that conception
of life which thinks scorn of the commonest of common things; they are the very substance of man's story.

But then also this simple sentence, read from An Affecting
another side, is one of the most moving in all the Sentence
Epistles of St. Paul. It shows us the great saint
and prophet exposed to a pathetic bodily need, and
anxious also, in those last days in the prison vault,
while a violent death is waiting for him outside its
door, to get back the books he loved. It was still
summer when he wrote. But winter would be
coming soon, in the large ancient sense of 'winter,'
when the equinoctial storms began; and he would
be bitterly cold, in common clothing, underground.
He had left a warm cloak, in Greek a *phelonê*, in Latin
a *pœnula*, behind him, at Troas, in the house of one

157

The Second Epistle to Timothy

2 Tim. iv.
13. Carpus, his friend; just possibly the house where
that memorable Eucharist was held (Acts xx. 7),
when Eutychus fell from the upper window. Perhaps
it was in that house that the persecutors had seized
him, to carry him for the last time to Rome; in the
ruthless hurry his travelling-cloak was left behind,
and also his books, some apparently of papyrus, but
some, and those the dearest to him (were they not
the scrolls of Holy Scripture, his stay and his joy?),
made of the costlier vellum. And he would fain *be
warm* while he yet lived, in that body emaciated with
sufferings. And he would fain *read* once more, even
with eyes dimmed by use and perhaps by disease,
but through which the deathless mind could still be
looking. So Timothy is to ask Carpus for the cloak,
and for the books, and to bring them with him.

Tindale's
Letter
    In a later age, in the sixteenth century, a re-
quest curiously similar was made by a true disciple
of St. Paul's, that great Christian and great English-
man, William Tindale, whose translation of the New
Testament is practically the basis of our versions
of to-day, Authorized and Revised. In 1535,
immured by the persecutor at Vilvorde, in Belgium,
he wrote, not long before his fiery martyrdom,
a Latin letter to the Marquis of Bergen, Governor
of the castle. 'I entreat your lordship, and that
by the Lord Jesus, that if I must remain here
for the winter you would beg the Commissary
to be so kind as to send me, from the things of
mine which he has, a warmer cap; I feel the cold
painfully in my head. Also a warmer cloak, for
the cloak I have is very thin. He has a woollen
shirt of mine, if he will send it. But most of all,

The Cloak and the Books

my Hebrew Bible, Grammar, and Vocabulary, that 2 Tim. iv. 13.
I may spend my time in that pursuit.'

Did the saints, each in his affliction, live to need
the warmth after all, and to need the books? As
to St. Paul we cannot know. He *may* have been
spared till 'winter,' and may have thankfully wrapt
the old friendly folds again round him, and bent over
the beloved books again. But it is more likely that
before that could happen he had passed through
death to life, and sunned himself in the light of the
Lord, and 'seen all knowledge' in His face.

However, the request stands here, legible for us. A 'Touch of Nature'
It touches the heart, age after age, with its strangely
simple intimation of human needs, bodily and mental,
in that life so natural amidst the supernatural. Is it
not also one of the surest of the many sure strokes
of internal witness to the authentic authorship of the
Epistle? I dare to say that the insertion of just such
a 'touch of nature' was, at that date, beyond the
finest conception of a fabricator. We feel, we see,
the veritable Paul in this simple verse; it is himself.

One note may be added as we leave the passage. A Note on Phelonê
Some expositors have suggested that the *phelonê*
was not a common cloak but a ceremonial one, a
'vestment'; that it was in fact a 'chasuble,' the
ephod-like robe worn at a later age in the ministry of
the Holy Communion, and to which the word *phelonê*
is as a fact applied. But the history of the term
makes this impossible. No certain use of *phelonê*
for a sacred vestment is discoverable for seven long
centuries after St. Paul's day. Just possibly the word
here may mean a *case for books*. But the far highest
probability makes it mean a cloak for common use.

43

ALEXANDER THE SMITH

2 Timothy 4: 14,15

ALEXANDER the coppersmith did me much evil: the Lord reward him according to his works: of whom be thou ware also; for he hath greatly withstood our words. A.V.

Alexander the smith wrought me (lit., *shewed me*) many a mischief; the Lord will requite him according to his works; *a man* against whom thou too must be on thy guard, for all too much did he withstand our discourses.

2 Tim. iv. 14, 15. A Note of Truth

AGAIN a personal reference is before us, and again it is one of the kind which makes an 'internal note' of truth in our precious Epistle—a reference so detached, so totally unlike a contrived allusion to known events or to a known person, that no antique fabricator would have devised it. Outside this passage we know literally nothing of this Alexander; no real reason connects him with the Alexander of 1 Tim. i. 20; possibly on purpose to *dis*connect him with that man, he is here called 'the coppersmith,' or more simply (so the word *chalceus* may be rendered) 'the smith,' perhaps a blacksmith. The words breathe unanxious fact and authenticity.

Alexander a Secret Enemy

We can only conjecture what the 'mischiefs' were which Alexander 'wrought,' and how he wrought them. It has been thought possible that he stood forward as St. Paul's open accuser, for the verb rendered 'wrought,' literally 'indicated,' bears sometimes the sense of indicting or accusing. But St. Paul never uses it so in the several other passages where it occurs in his writings. And in this passage, if I understand it, the suggestion is far rather that Alexander was *a secret* enemy, a wolf clothed in a fleece, a pretended disciple, who used his intimacy to play the traitor and entrap the saint to his doom. For we observe that St. Paul takes care here to warn Timothy against him; he is to be 'on his guard against him'; words which would hardly be in place if the man were notoriously on the pagan side. I seem to see in him a feigned enquirer, perhaps a feigned convert, very likely in the pay of the persecutor; he seems to seek the Gospel, but he really hates it, and, once out of hearing, 'withstands all too much' the 'discourses' which Paul and Timothy held with their visitors or their congregations. He is either a pagan all the time, or more possibly one of those bitter Judaistic enemies of the Pauline Gospel whose malice may well have gone the length of giving the Apostle up to the emissaries of Nero, in some moment of seeming security and concealment, if thus they might be rid for ever of the detested doctrine.

Well might Timothy 'be on his guard' when next Alexander should present himself, under the disguise of friendship, or of spiritual curiosity, meaning 'many a mischief' all the while.

'The Lord shall requite him according to his works.' The Authorized Version reads, 'The Lord *reward* him,' not, '*shall reward* him;' making the Apostle to express the desire, the

2 Tim. iv. 14, 15.

The Prediction of Retribution

The Second Epistle to Timothy

prayer, that retribution may overtake this enemy. But the right reading, beyond reasonable question, demands the insertion of 'shall,' and leaves us with the Apostle's mere affirmation that retribution will find Alexander out. And even this, we may be sure, would be said with the implication that the retribution should take place only if Alexander should prove impenitent; let him change his mind, let him renounce his merciless treacheries and seek pardon from the offended Christ, and he should find the promised welcome, full and free. St. Paul does but proclaim the unalterable law that the impenitent sinner, by the deepest necessities of spiritual life and order, *must* sooner or later be 'rewarded according to his works.'

Would it be a real mercy to the impenitent sinner himself if it were otherwise? No, surely. The scourge of God is the very implement of His compassion if it awakes the sinning soul to its self-wrought misery before it is too late to escape a final doom.

Prayers for Retribution Meanwhile do not let us hastily think that there is a moral discord in those solemn prayers and appeals for retribution which are scattered over Scripture. They are frequent in the Psalms, and here and there they occur in the tender-spirited Jeremiah's pages. And they meet us also, though much more rarely, in the New Testament itself. Even in the mysterious visions of the Revelation the martyr-souls are heard (Rev. vi. 10) asking how long the vengeance on their murderers is to be delayed; a passage no doubt profoundly symbolical, but none the less sufficient to assure us that a sinless cry for retribution is a morally possible thing. 2 Tim. iv. 14, 15.

It is possible for the sanctified human spirit so to see the awfulness of wrong-doing, and its antagonism to God, as to be impelled, without sin, even to cry out and pray for a just retribution ; no angry clamour of a bitter personal rancour, but the voice of angered conscience.

Yet is there 'a more excellent way,' more excellent at least for us when nothing is assailed *but ourselves.* 'Father, forgive them;' 'Lord, lay not this sin to their charge.'

44

ALONE, BUT WITH THE LORD

2 Timothy 4: 16,17

AT my first answer no man stood with me, but all men forsook me : *I pray God* that it may not be laid to their charge. Notwithstanding the Lord stood with me. A.V.

When I first spoke in my defence no one supported me, but they all left me in the lurch ; may it not be reckoned against them ! But the Lord stood beside me.

**2 Tim. iv.
16, 17.
A Wish of
Pardon and
Love**

ALREADY St. Paul is taking here that other tone of which we spoke just above. Is he not consciously echoing a certain dying voice which never, in all his life, could he have forgotten, the last prayer but one of Stephen (Acts vii. 60), while the stones were beating out his soul, and 'the young man named Saul' was keeping the clothes of the slayers ; 'Lord, lay not this sin to their charge'? The once stern Sanhedrist, he who 'was consenting' to Stephen's death, is now the aged labourer and sufferer for Stephen's blessed Lord, only waiting the signal to follow Stephen 'without the gate' to die. In this his last hour of need that awful form of suffering falls on his wounded heart—desertion, the abandonment of him by all who might have supported his heart by legal skill or faithful sympathy. And he meets it only with this prayer, 'May it not be reckoned to them!'

Alexander the smith was the ruthless foe of the Gospel; his crime will be punished. These were weak wills and faint hearts; may they be gently handled by their Judge!

164

Alone, but with the Lord

'When I first spoke in my defence.' The evident 2 Tim. iv. 16, 17. allusion is to the opening of his trial at Rome, the *prima actio*, the first proceedings. St. Paul's was The Course of the Trial no doubt a highly important case in the eyes of the imperial officials. This man was a leader of long standing among the Christians, who were now widely believed to be the most profane of *atheists*, (for who ever saw their Gods?) and the most dangerous enemies of society and of the state. This man, many would remember, had been in the Roman courts before; his case had occupied them, at intervals, for two whole years. To be sure he had been released; but although legal proofs of guilt had failed, had not strange things been said about his profound fanaticism? Had not a dangerous magnetism played around him, a power to draw other men into absurd and monstrous beliefs and hopes? With so much smoke there must be fire enough to kindle even a literal conflagration! So the fanatical leader must be deliberately and severely examined, day after day, charge after charge; a whole world of conspiracies might be detected in the process.

The *prima actio* accordingly was taken, and now Prima Actio it was over. St. Paul had spoken in his own defence; for no principle of faith or love bade him hold his tongue under accusations which involved not only his own good name but that of his Lord and of the Church. And then the case was adjourned. In the dialect of Roman law there was an *ampliatio*. Ampliatio The prisoner was remanded.

'No one supported me.' The Roman system allowed the accused the use of 'advocates,' that is to say, skilled lawyers 'called to the side' (*ad-vocati*)

The Second Epistle to Timothy

of the man at the bar. The term included alike solicitors and barristers, as we should distinguish them; and when, in his first imprisonment, the Apostle had sought such help, as we may assume he did, doubtless he found it ready to his hand, for that time was not a reign of terror, and he was an interesting figure, perhaps almost a popular figure, in Roman circles. But all was altered now. To take the part of this man now as his legal 'advocate' might cost barrister or solicitor his whole prospects; indeed it might cost him a silent removal, by the secret agents of the despot, from society, from life. He would have seemed to take open part with a man suspected of disloyalty.

The Apostle without an Advocate

So the help of men of law was asked in vain; it was not convenient, it was not possible, in this particular case, even when former acquaintanceship was appealed to. The old, broken, apparently wrecked and disappointed man, must needs do for himself what he best could, in this his uttermost hour, with all the world against him.

He 'was a man of like feelings' with us. To be forsaken thus was very bitter to his human heart, a heart which must have found itself not a little hungry just then for sympathy and help.

'But the Lord'

'But the LORD stood beside him.' Wonderful 'but'! It points us to an infinite counterpoise to that dreadful weight of desolate forsakenness. He was not alone. JESUS was with him, in the court-house, at the bar, before the unjust judges. In HIS company, St. Paul could think and act in the power of a great tranquillity. How, in that power, he could also *speak*, we shall presently see.

45

THE COURT-HOUSE AND THE TRIAL

2 Timothy 4: 17

NOTWITHSTANDING the Lord stood with me, and strengthened me ; that by me the preaching might be fully known, and that all the Gentiles might hear : and I was delivered out of the mouth of the lion. A.V.

But the Lord stood by me, and gave me power, so that through me the proclamation might be made in full, and that the Gentiles might hear it ; and I was rescued out of the lion's mouth.

THIS verse, duly considered, paints for us one of the *2 Tim. iv. 17.* great pictures of the Bible. The picture happens to be preserved, if we may put it so, in a remote corner *A Great Picture* of the wonderful Scripture gallery. This closing paragraph of St. Paul's dying Letter is not one of those prominent passages which are more or less familiar to every Christian. To many a true believer and careful reader it is a nook not often visited ; when visited, it is perhaps too quickly traversed to allow its treasure to be fully seen. But the treasure is great and rare Let us to-day pause in the place awhile, and look deliberately around. This scene is a noble one indeed.

We have pondered already, in our last reading, *The Present* that glorious central light which gives life to the *Lord* whole picture, 'But the Lord stood by me.' Yes, whatever else the event presents to the spiritual eye, it shows us this — JESUS present with His saint, mysteriously, specially, 'giving him power.' The aged one, worn low by labour, suffering, and many

The Second Epistle to Timothy

sorrows, is not really left alone there to his own feebleness. Two are standing there, not one, 'and the form of the Second is like the Son of God.' He stands, embracing the man whom He has loved and saved, pouring by His touch an immortal force into that weary head and heart, and that fragile frame.

The Place and Audience

But while the spiritual eye can see this, guided by the words of the Epistle, the natural eye is helpless to follow it. What do our mere senses see? On the one hand a vast concourse, spectators and auditors, all full of the curiosity which a remarkable trial has always excited, above all a trial which has life or death for its issues, and more than ever when the accusation connects itself with the 'sensation' of an alleged public danger. Men and women, they crowd the court-house, a mighty multitude of 'Gentiles,' that is to say, of the pagan population of the Capital. The building where we find them can without difficulty be imagined in outline, for it is one of those *basilicas* whose interior arrangements became the model for the first churches of the Christian Empire; many of them were actually converted, just as they stood, into such churches. Place before your eyes the Madeleine at Paris, for example, with its stately oblong, and you see a fair suggestion of the shape and design of the building where St. Paul answered for his life. It had its nave, and also its aisles, parted by pillars from the nave. Along the aisles ran galleries, to give room for the throngs which sought admission on such a day as this. At the far end was an apse. Within it stood a raised platform, the 'tribunal,' supporting the chairs of the judge and

168

The Court-House and the Trial

his assessors. Behind this were seats, ranged along 2 Tim. iv. 17. the wall of the apse. In front of it, guarded by lictors, stood the accused, and the accuser or accusers were placed near him.

On that tribunal who sits to-day, to hear this Nero momentous case argued? Quite possibly the Emperor himself. See, he has entered from the Palace with his body - guard, and has taken his place; it is none other than Nero. The face was once handsome, perhaps once noble, but that awful change has passed over it which seems almost fatally, almost mechanically, to come into a nature, not quite true and virtuous, called to the tremendous temptations of really absolute power; practically irresponsible, intoxicated by the possibilities opened before a flattered and unlimited self-will. The stain of an advanced sensuality lies upon the features, which yet look as if once capable of higher thoughts and a fine ideal. The frown, almost the scowl, of a growing cruelty, born of a universal subservience, sits upon the forehead as the judge surveys the audience and looks down upon the Accused.

The Accused—we have seen him already. He The Accused stands there, to all seeming, totally alone; broken down in physical respects, without a single friend, and loaded with charges of private and public wickedness which make 'the Gentiles' wonder at him as a monster. And now those charges are being stated in the pleadings of the accusing 'orator.' These completed, as no 'orator' takes the part of the prisoner to-day, he will have to reply for himself, if reply he can.

46

THE CHARGE

2 Timothy 4: 17

THAT by me the preaching might be fully known, and that all the Gentiles might hear : and I was delivered out of the mouth of the lion. A.V.

So that through me the proclamation might be made in full, and that all the Gentiles might hear ; and I was rescued out of the lion's mouth.

2 Tim. iv. 17.
What was the Accusation

IT is of course impossible to say with decision and in detail what were the crimes alleged that day against St. Paul. But knowing what we do of the general attitude of the popular mind of the period towards the Christians, the thoughts which ignorance conceived, and which a calculating malice sedulously fostered, we shall not be far astray if we say that they were almost entirely political. No doubt they carried a strong tincture of religious suspicion in them. It would be urged that the accused had spoken against the Gods, and had discouraged their worship. As a Jew, he would not be regarded as profane because he did not personally adore Jupiter or Diana ; the strange faith of the Jew, who endured no image of his mysterious God, was a *relligio licita,* a 'legalized religion.' But this Jew was a Christian also. And Christians were known not only to abstain from the worship of Jupiter but openly to preach that Jupiter was no God ; which was another matter altogether. Aye, and they were known to hold also that it was wrong to adore the Emperor ;

and this was a tenet even more strange and 2 Tim. iv. formidable than the denial of the Olympian Powers. 17. For the imperial idea at Rome had developed itself into a religious shape in which the political elements were inextricably woven into the mystical. To the Emperor must now be paid not only homage but worship. He was, as it were, the incarnate Genius of Rome. And to refuse to own him as such, what could it mean? What could lie behind it but a deep disloyalty to the imperial idea itself? The The Suspicion of Political Disloyalty man who took that attitude was a dangerous element in society and in the State. His creed was anarchism. In the phrase of a great Latin historian, who saw Christianity only from the outside and with a cynical suspicion, it was 'a hatred of the human race.'

Not least among the trials of the saints in that early A peculiar Trial to Faith and Feeling day, and in many a time of persecution since that day, even till now, must have been the pain of having to feel that they were accused and condemned, in large measure, at least as to *the form* of the matter, upon grounds quite alien from the real point at issue. In their own inmost souls the whole question was one of spiritual fidelity to the Lord Jesus Christ. If it were not for HIM, and for all that 'HE was given to them to be,' they would scarcely be there at all, standing before a persecuting tribunal, facing a sentence of death. If the accusation could only take the precise form that they were worshippers of 'one JESUS,' and that He was evil—the issue would have been absolutely clear; it would have been a simple thing, however awful in its sequel, to reply that He was infinitely good, and that they would readily die

The Second Epistle to Timothy

2 Tim. iv.
17.
Polycarp

to affirm His infinite goodness. Thus it sometimes
was, as when, about a century after St. Paul,
holy Polycarp at Smyrna was asked point blank
to 'rail at Christ,' and then made that immortal
answer; 'Eighty and six years I have served Him,
and He never did me wrong; how shall I rail at my
King who saved me?' But much more often the
martyr s soul was perplexed and troubled by having
to meet death upon, nominally, quite other grounds;
social, political, or what not. Just so it was in

China

China, in the year of Christ 1900. Saint upon saint
was murdered in that time of terror not, upon the
surface, for holiness' sake but for the sake of a
supposed unpatriotic complicity with 'the foreigner,'
a treachery to China.

A Supreme
Fidelity

Great and wonderful was the victory, because a
victory won amidst so complicated a 'fiery trial,'
when the confessor of the name of Jesus was true to
his Lord, even to the endurance of a terrible death,
without the uplifting consciousness in his soul that
the world perfectly understood that he was dying to
seal his spiritual faith in a sinless Saviour, whom the
world might hate, but before whom also it must stand
in awe. To refuse, for Christ's sake, the small con-
cession that would send the man away unscathed,
while he knew all the while that 'the Gentiles'
regarded him as a mere social peril—this was fidelity
indeed.

Such probably was the pain present to the heart
of St. Paul as he stood that day in the Basilica.
But wait awhile, and we shall hear him, as his
unseen Master uplifts him, mind and soul, telling the
thronging audience what is, after all, *the fact* of his
position.   172

47

THE DEFENCE

2 Timothy 4: 17,18

THAT by me the preaching might be fully known, and that all the Gentiles might hear : and I was delivered out of the mouth of the lion. And the Lord shall deliver me from every evil work, and will preserve me unto his heavenly kingdom : to whom be glory for ever and ever. Amen. A.V.

So that through me the proclamation might be made in full, and that all the Gentiles might hear : and I was rescued out of the lion's mouth. The Lord will rescue me from every evil work, and will bring me safe into His kingdom, His heavenly kingdom : to whom be the glory unto the ages of the ages. Amen.

WE are still watching the scene in the great Basilica, probably one of the many structures which crowded with their magnificence that space so curiously narrow, compared with what it once contained of both material and moral importance, the Forum of Rome. The accuser, the accomplished barrister, has spoken, and called for a sentence adverse to the prisoner. We seem to hear the movements and the suppressed talk of the audience, as the tension of listening is over ; possibly even exclamations of hatred and alarm are breaking out, directed towards this forsaken old man yonder at the bar. *2 Tim. iv. 17, 18. The Scene*

But now he speaks, his own counsel in his own defence. It was not an easy matter to win complete attention ; an angrily prejudiced multitude is no good listener. And here was a person whose nationality, age, and supposed antecedents, were all greatly against *The Accused Speaks*

The Second Epistle to Timothy

his speaking with success. Moreover, as we gather
from certain Letters of his written years before, he
had some special physical d'fficulties to contend with,
such as to give embittered opponents a certain *excuse*
for saying that 'his bodily presence was weak and
his speech contemptible' (2 Cor. x. 10).

He begins; we seem as we listen to hear him
uttering at first his phrases with an accent of labour.
But as he proceeds the voice gets power, and the fire
of a strange eloquence burns in the sentences. This
is very far from his first public address under accusation; he has spoken before, on the steps of the castle
at Jerusalem, and at the tribunal of Festus at Cæsarea;
and then certainly his 'speech' was not 'contemptible.' He is one of those who on common occasions
may be troubled by nervous weakness, but in a great
hour, not least in a formidable hour, rise above themselves, or rather rise to their true and full selves as
God has made them. And besides—there is that
wonderful Friend at his side, 'giving him power,'
touching his whole being with a divine magnetism
for this one last effort in His own beloved Name.

**He deals
with the
Charges**
At first, we may suppose, the old Apostle dealt—
for the honour of the Gospel, and of the Lord, yes,
and for his own fair fame as a true man; for no man
is asked by grace to treat lightly his own moral
reputation—with the charges that day urged against
him. And his own words here enable us to say that
he did so with victorious effect. Partly by convincing
appeals to fact and to reason, but also surely by the
mighty logic of the manifestation of a personality
true and great throughout, he appears to have

174

The Defence

secured, even at that tribunal, where, let us 2 Tim. iv.
remember, even under Nero, the Roman reverence
for law was not quite absent, a favourable award.
At least there was a suspense of judgment. It was
impossible to condemn him then and there. He 'was
rescued out of the lion's mouth,'—as we should say, out
of 'the jaws of death,' a death only postponed, to be
sure, yet postponed long enough to let him witness
yet awhile, if only in this last precious Letter, till the
hour not of Nero's will but of the Lord's should
strike.

But then this was not all, nor nearly all. His 'The
defence was a minor matter. He recognized that Proclam-ation'
here was given him one more opportunity, one last
'open door,' wide and wonderful, for that 'testimony of JESUS' for which he had lived so long.
And he seized it with all his soul, and 'the Spirit
gave him utterance.' 'The proclamation was
made in full, and all the Gentiles heard.' O for a
report by faithful Luke of that great 'proclamation,'
spoken—and so spoken that a dead silence gave it
way—before judge, and assessors, and accusers, and
the crowds of listeners in nave, and aisle, and gallery,
and apse! But of its main burthen we may be quite
sure, with the Acts and the Epistles before us. It
was CHRIST JESUS, in all His sacred glory of Person,
Work, and Love. If Paul was named at all it was
only as the monument and example of His mercy.
CHRIST was the theme; and the awe-struck audience
passed away at last, in instances uncounted, to
think of Him and to feel after Him. 'That day'
shall shew the fruits of that last great bearing of the

Name, before the Gentiles and their kings, by the Chosen Vessel.

As for him, he was carried back once more to prison. But it was in an inward liberty more large and full than ever. 'The ages of the ages' were before him, and through them all his Redeemer would love him and would keep him, and 'the glory' should be His.

48

LAST MESSAGES

2 Timothy 4: 19-22

SALUTE Prisca and Aquila, and the household of Onesiphorus. Erastus abode at Corinth : but Trophimus have I left at Miletum sick. Do thy diligence to come before winter. Eubulus greeteth thee, and Pudens, and Linus, and Claudia, and all the brethren. The Lord Jesus Christ be with thy spirit. Grace be with you. Amen. A.V.

Salute Prisca, and Aquila, and Onesiphorus' house. Erastus stayed at Corinth ; Trophimus I left at Miletus, ill. Do thy very best to come before winter. There greets thee Eubulus, and Pudens, and Linus, and Claudia, and the brethren all.
The Lord be with thy spirit. Grace be with you. Amen.

WE come to the last lines of the dying Letter. Let us treat them as simply as possible ; the deep, the sacred human interest of them, human, but full of the message of God to the inmost soul, will gain nothing by elaboration.   **2 Tim. iv. 19-22. The Close**

True to his familiar methods of address the Apostle dictates a few personal greetings and details before he ends. Two dear friends of many years are present to his affectionate heart ; they were then at Ephesus, apparently ; Timothy could visit them. Prisca must be greeted, and Aquila, the now fast ageing companions of his life ; true, self-sacrificing (see Rom. xvi. 3), absolutely sympathetic in faith and hope ; they will not be long behind him on the immortal shore. Then there is Onesiphorus' family. He has thought of them earlier in the letter, and has invoked 'mercy' upon their heads ; now he wishes them to receive his   **Personal Messages**

177

The Second Epistle to Timothy

2 Tim. iv. 19-22.
direct personal salutation, for their father's dear sake and their own. Next he thinks of those who were, or who might be, around him, and for whose greetings Timothy would look. Two well-tried friends were absent, whose presence Timothy might apparently assume. Erastus—possibly the Christian city-treasurer of Corinth (Rom. xvi. 23), a man of whom we would gladly know more, but more probably the faithful *chaplain*, if we may call him so, of Acts xix. 22—had been with St. Paul when he was seized (so we may infer), and had contrived to keep near him as far as Corinth, but there had stayed behind. Earlier on the sad voyage, at Miletus, the port sacred with the memories of the Farewell of Acts xx. 17, another friend, who would have accompanied him to Rome had it been possible, had been taken ill and compelled to stay; it was Trophimus, the Asian Christian (Acts xx. 4, xxi. 29), his companion and attendant on his last visit to Jerusalem. But although these were away there was still a little circle able to find entrance on occasion to the dungeon, and to share with the always present Luke the sacred privilege of cheering the solitude of St. Paul. Eubulus was one; and there was Pudens, and Linus; and other 'brethren' were within reach. With them one woman is grouped, Claudia, bearing the clan-name of the imperial House, though this is no sure evidence for what is in itself unlikely, in the total absence of any such tradition, her relationship to the Cæsars. Singularly enough there is a bare, an almost vanishing, possibility, too subtle for discussion here, that she was *a Briton*, daughter of the British king Cogidubnus,

Absent Friends

Present Friends

178

whose capital was what we know now as Chichester. **2 Tim. iv. 19-22.**
And there is the like thin shadow of support for a
conjecture that the Pudens mentioned just before
was a Roman gentleman who, so a complimentary
poem of Martial's informs us, married a British
Claudia, a wedding of interest at the time in Roman
society.   But nothing can well be more frail than
the evidence for the surmise here mentioned, and the
names lie before us with only this for our certainty
about them, but this is inestimable, that they are
names of members of the family of God, and that we
shall, in our Father's mercy, see them hereafter with
our Elder Brother in the eternal home.   More solid,
for early tradition favours it, and there lies no difficulty in the way, is the belief that the Linus here
named is the first Christian pastor to be entrusted
with the bishopric of Rome in the early and holy
simplicity of that great office, with its frequent calls
to martyrdom.   Yet even here the more certain and
more fruitful reflection is simply this, that Linus,
with Paul, and Timothy, 'and the brethren all,' was
'a man in CHRIST.'

So the letter closes.   Only two last messages **The Final Words**
remain for our reverent notice, one from the human
heart, the other from the grace of God. 'Do thy
very best to come before winter'; pathetic sentence,
breaking in upon the friends' dear names and the
mention of the missing invalid ; a sentence the actual
answer to which God only knows.   Then in conclusion, to Timothy first, and finally to the disciples

The Second Epistle to Timothy

2 Tim. iv.
19-22. with him—for we note the closing plural, '*you*'—
there comes a living benediction to complete the
dying Letter. St. Paul invokes the presence of the
beloved Saviour, abiding close to the very 'spirit' of
his longed-for correspondent, and he asks that the
power of the eternal grace may follow him and
his :—'THE LORD BE WITH THY SPIRIT. GRACE
BE WITH YOU ALL. AMEN.'